Visions of England

Poems selected by The Earl of Burford

JOHN HUNT PUBLISHING

First published by O-Books, 2019
O-Books is an imprint of John Hunt Publishing Ltd., No. 3 East St., Alresford, Hampshire SO24 9EE, UK
office@jhpbooks.net
www.johnhuntpublishing.com
www.o-books.com

For distributor details and how to order please visit the 'Ordering' section on our website.

ISBN: 978 1 78904 048 7
978 1 78904 049 4 (ebook)
Library of Congress Control Number: 2018934825

Design: Stuart Davies

UK: Printed and bound by CPI Group (UK) Ltd, Croydon, CR0 4YY
US: Printed and bound by Thomson-Shore, 7300 West Joy Road, Dexter, MI 48130

We operate a distinctive and ethical publishing philosophy in all areas of our business, from our global network of authors to production and worldwide distribution.

Visions of England

Poems selected by The Earl of Burford

Nicholas Hagger

BOOKS

Winchester, UK
Washington, USA

Also by Nicholas Hagger

The Fire and the Stones
Selected Poems
The Universe and the Light
A White Radiance
A Mystic Way
Awakening to the Light
A Spade Fresh with Mud
The Warlords
Overlord
A Smell of Leaves and Summer
The Tragedy of Prince Tudor
The One and the Many
Wheeling Bats and a Harvest Moon
The Warm Glow of the Monastery Courtyard
The Syndicate
The Secret History of the West
The Light of Civilization
Classical Odes
Overlord, one-volume edition
Collected Poems 1958 – 2005
Collected Verse Plays
Collected Stories
The Secret Founding of America
The Last Tourist in Iran
The Rise and Fall of Civilizations
The New Philosophy of Universalism
The Libyan Revolution
Armageddon
The World Government
The Secret American Dream
A New Philosophy of Literature
A View of Epping Forest
My Double Life 1: This Dark Wood
My Double Life 2: A Rainbow over the Hills

Selected Stories: Follies and Vices of the Modern Elizabethan Age
Selected Poems: Quest for the One
The Dream of Europa
Life Cycle and Other New Poems 2006 – 2016
The First Dazzling Chill of Winter
The Secret American Destiny
Peace for our Time
World State
World Constitution
King Charles the Wise

The front cover is a photograph of Nicholas Hagger shown in imaginative vision by the 17th-century cottage believed to be the "dwelling" of Wordsworth's Solitary, Blea Tarn House between Little Langdale and Great Langdale in England's Lake District, on 14 April 1986.

⌐Symbol

A corner-mark (⌐) at the beginning of the line denotes that there is a break or gap before that line which has been obscured because it falls at the bottom of a page.

CONTENTS

Indexes

Preface to *Visions of England*:
The Visionary Tradition

Meaning of 'Visions' and 'Visionary'
A 'vision' is "something which is apparently seen otherwise than by ordinary sight; especially an appearance of a prophetic or mystical character, or having the nature of a revelation, supernaturally presented to the mind in sleep or in an abnormal state"; or "a mental concept of a distinct or vivid kind; a highly imaginative scheme or anticipation"; or "the action or fact of seeing or contemplating something not actually present to the eye; mystical or supernatural insight or foresight" (*Shorter Oxford English Dictionary*). ('A revelation' is, according to the same dictionary, "the disclosure of knowledge to man by a divine or supernatural agency".)

'Visions of England' therefore means "views of places in England which are also seen otherwise than by ordinary sight, with prophetic, mystical, revelatory and imaginative insight, not by the bodily eye". Or more simply "seeing England with prophetic, mystical, revelatory and imaginative insight".

'Visionary' means "able or accustomed to see visions; capable of receiving impressions by means of visions"; or "presented or apprehended in a vision"; or "existing in imagination only" (*Shorter Oxford English Dictionary*). The 'visionary tradition' in poetry is therefore "the tradition of seeing visions and reflecting them, and imaginative vision, in poems".

These poems, all written before 1999, are views of England filled with prophecy and mysticism and looking back to the work of the Metaphysical poets and the visionary tradition of Blake.

Provenance of this selection: places in England
On 20 February 1979 I visited the English Neoclassical literary critic Christopher Ricks, then Professor of English Literature at Cambridge University, in Christ's College, Cambridge to discuss my early Metaphysical poems, which he had been reading. He gave me a tutorial and rattled through sixteen points on the poems for two hours and

then said, "There are too many poems. Get a friend to make a selection of 30 and bring them out, and make your *entrée*." Having edited his definitive *The Poems of Tennyson* (1969), he advised me to follow Tennyson's practice of amending lines, advice I took to heart and have implemented ever since. He then took me for lunch in Christ's Senior Common Room. I sat next to him at a long table among a dozen dons.

I was in a creative time and more poems kept coming, and I was still working full-time and coping with my new poems in the evenings and at weekends. My lengthy *Selected Poems: A Metaphysical's Way of Fire* (146 poems or excerpts) came out in 1991, followed by my *Collected Poems: A White Radiance*, 1958–1993 in 1994 (1,272 poems), and – following a further visit to Christopher Ricks on 27 January 1993 and a day walking round Oxford with him on 21 June 1993 – my first epic poem *Overlord* about the Second World War from D-Day to the Fall of Berlin (41,000 lines of blank verse in four separate volumes, 1995–1997). And I wrote two verse plays. There were now even more poems along with works of epic and dramatic verse, and I had still done nothing about getting a friend to select 30. I thought John Ezard of *The Guardian* might assume that role, but he was busy writing articles and meeting deadlines and we met increasingly infrequently.

In March 1998 the Earl of Burford, the heir to the Dukedom of St Albans, became my Literary Secretary following an interview at my then home in Albion Hill, Loughton which doubled up as Head Office of the Oak-Tree Group of Schools. He worked five days a week at Otley Hall in Suffolk, a historic Tudor house I had acquired and opened to the public, and I drove down twice a week to oversee the restoration and running of the stately home and work with him. His ancestor the 3rd Earl of Southampton, Shakespeare's patron, had been closely involved with the Earl of Essex, whose secretary Robert Gosnold III had owned it and lived there, and with his Cambridge friend Bartholomew Gosnold, Robert Gosnold III's nephew. Both Southampton and Bartholomew Gosnold had joined Essex's Cádiz and Azores expeditions in 1596 and 1597 – Southampton had captained Essex's ship on the second of these – and Southampton had funded Bartholomew Gosnold's expedition to America in 1602, which had been planned at Otley Hall and during which Bartholomew named Martha's Vineyard (after his daughter

Martha) and Cape Cod. So Otley Hall had strong family associations for the Earl of Burford. A full account of Otley Hall's historical and literary associations can be found in my illustrated guidebook *Otley Hall* (2001), which can still be obtained at the property.

At one of our early meetings in my study, which had been an Elizabethan tiring-room (or attiring-room, dressing-room) for travelling players, the Earl of Burford remarked, "Your work is like a cathedral amid modern buildings." I told him about the need for a new selection and the idea emerged in our discussions that he would select 100 poems, not 30, focusing on places in England featured in my poems and on my metaphysical perspective. As my Literary Secretary he read all my poetic works.

Principles, thought processes and categories behind selection
On 30 April 1999 the Earl of Burford messaged me that he had selected 152 poems, mostly from *Collected Poems: A White Radiance* and a few from what would become *Classical Odes*. Under the heading 'Poems: British Selection' he set out the principles and thought processes behind his selection:

> I have selected 152 poems, some long, some short, some very short, from which I shall make a final selection of about 100 next week. I shall also put them in order, according to what scheme I'm not yet sure. I am tempted, however, to begin with 'Elemental Sea' because it contains the image of the hermit, which I think should be the defining symbol of the selection.
>
> You, the poet, are the hermit. You give your readers a tour of Britain, guiding them by the light of your metaphysical lamp. Like a hermit of old, you tramp the length and breadth of the country, teaching the mystic tradition. Suddenly you light on an ancient stone and holding your lamp over it cry, "Look here! See, see!"
>
> Thus you cast yourself in the role of psychopomp [in Greek mythology, "a conductor of souls to the place of the dead" (*Shorter Oxford English Dictionary*) and so a spiritual guide for the souls of the living]; or of the shaman, willing – by a huge

effort of mind – his country's renewal.

One of the advantages of using the image of the hermit at the very beginning is that it lets the reader know that there is a vital exchange between mind and landscape. The mind's ecstatic charges not only apprehend the landscape, they vivify it. For this reason, I've also been keen to include poems that open a window on the landscape of the poet's mind, as for example 'Bumble-Bee: Correspondence'.

Included also are poems whose central images are symbols of Britain and British life: the sea, the oak tree, bluebells in spring, the snail etc. All these help to give insights into the peculiar spiritual life of the country. In addition, it makes sense that certain images that are both powerful and intrinsic to the poet's metaphoric world (e.g. a tree as the universe) should recur in the selection. Ultimately, then, a metaphysical vision of the country emerges.

The overall impression should be of a poet with a strong sense of Britain's special destiny – the country, after all, that has fostered his own special insights into the universe.

In the event he did not begin with 'Elemental Sea' or include 'Bumble-Bee: Correspondence'. Among the papers is his handwritten list of the 152 poems with strike-throughs to bring the tally down to 101 (in fact 102 as one of his numbers merges two poems).

He also identified 26 poetic categories in the poems in *Collected Poems: A White Radiance* and what would become *Classical Odes*, which he considered for the selection:

England; Britain; English Heritage/History; British Heritage/History; Essex; Cornwall; East Anglia; The Celtic World; Europe; The Sea; The Far East; The Middle East; Decline of the West; Christian Culture; Greece/Rome/Classical Culture; History; The Modern Age; World Politics; Gardens; Love; Death; Nature; The Spiritual Quest; Mysticism; The Artist and his Art (The Imagination); The Fire/Light.

It is for the reader to judge how many of these categories can be found in the poems he chose, but his focus on England excluded many of the categories beyond England's shores.

There is a later note in my handwriting among these papers: "Call it *Visions of England*?"

Visions of England was the outcome: 102 poems celebrating places in England and my metaphysical outlook. These were in fact universal – indeed Universalist – poems with a significance that went far beyond England's borders.

Visions of England, then, covers what was in 1999 about one-thirteenth and is now about one-twentieth of my poetic works (excluding my two epics and five verse plays), and sees me as a hermit. I should point out that a later selection, *Selected Poems: Quest for the One* (211 poems or excerpts, 2015), sees me as a quester for Reality and observer of social follies and vices in all my poetic works, and that it would be possible to see me in a different light in a different one-twentieth of my poetic works: for example, as a journeyer along the Mystic Way (as in *Selected Poems: A Metaphysical's Way of Fire*); as a developing Universalist; as a poet within the perspective and tradition of seven disciplines; as a social, satirical poet; as a reflector of Western culture; as a Nature poet; as a war poet of the Second World War, Iraq and Afghanistan; and as a poet carrying forward the tradition of the Metaphysical poets in Baroque work that unites sense and spirit, the Augustan and Romantic perspectives. *Visions of England* may include aspects of all of these eight alternative approaches, but the point I am making is that it would be possible for a selection of a similar length to offer a completely different view of my poetic works.

Overtaken by events

Visions of England was overtaken by events. In 1998 I had written a verse play, *The Tragedy of Prince Tudor*, about a Prince who protests against the impending break-up of the United Kingdom by hostile international forces, and the prospect of the loss of its sovereignty. Dismayed at the Blair Government's Reform Bill to abolish the hereditary peers' voting rights in the House of Lords and end a 700-year-old tradition, the Earl of Burford told me he detected Brussels' hand at work and was going to protest.

As a descendant of Shakespeare's patron the 3rd Earl of Southampton (and also of the 17th Earl of Oxford who Oxfordians regard as Shakespeare, and of Charles II and Nell Gwyn), and mindful of Southampton's involvement in the Earl of Essex's march through London and abortive *coup* of 1601 that led to Southampton's imprisonment in the Tower and Essex's execution (and Robert Gosnold III's being fined £40), he felt he had to rise to his family's tradition of making a stand in critical times and make a similar protest in what would be a "beautiful act" that would also be remembered for 400 years. He told me he was planning to climb onto the throne in the House of Lords, stand on its seat and address the assembled peers. I talked him out of violating the seat of the throne.

On 26 October 1999 he went ahead and made a principled protest in a packed House of Lords by leaping onto the Woolsack, the Lord Chancellor's wool-stuffed seat, and denouncing the Third Reading of the Reform Bill, which he branded treasonous. His speech would today be regarded as anti-EU: "This Bill, drafted in Brussels, is treason. What we are witnessing is the abolition of Britain.... No Queen, no culture, no sovereignty, no freedom." His spirited "act" led to 92 hereditary peers remaining in the Lords to this day, of whom 90 are now elected.

In a further protest the Earl of Burford stood for Parliament in a by-election. He left my employ in April 2000 and then changed his name to Charles Beauclerk. In August 2000 my publisher went into receivership and the manuscript was put away. It was soon buried under other papers.

Nearly twenty years later, in January 2018, I was assembling papers for my next deposit in my literary Archive at the Albert Sloman Library, University of Essex and came across *Visions of England*. As a celebration of places in England it looked perfect for the UK's post-Brexit time. I immediately saw that my poetic treatment of the places reflected aspects of England's history and culture. I contacted Charles Beauclerk and he gave his blessing to the selection's remaining under the byline of 'the Earl of Burford' as he had still been known as the Earl of Burford when he made the selection. I am delighted that *Visions of England* can at last see the light of day.

Shakespeare asked the 3rd Earl of Southampton to support his poems 'Venus and Adonis' and 'The Rape of Lucrece' in two letters/dedications written in 1593 and 1594 (the only letters by Shakespeare that have survived, both written to the 3rd Earl of Southampton), and just over 400 years later the 3rd Earl of Southampton's descendant made a selection of my poems in Tudor Otley Hall, which Southampton is thought to have visited. Of the many remarkable events that have happened in my life, this is one of the more extraordinary.

In the visionary tradition of the Metaphysical poets; Blake; and Shelley

My "visions" are rooted in the 17th-century Metaphysical poets, especially Marvell – as can be seen in 'A Metaphysical in Marvell's Garden'.

The title *Visions of England* echoes volume 12 of my poetic works, *Visions Near the Gates of Paradise*, and looks back to Blake's "fourfold vision" (for example, in my 'Beauty and Angelhood'); to his critique of the materialist outlook in his letter to Butts in 1802, "May God us keep/From Single vision & Newton's sleep"; and to his 'Visions of the Daughters of Albion' ('Albion' being another word for 'England' and the name of the road in which I then lived). I must point out that Blake's daughters' visions were troubled whereas my visions were in harmony with Nature and the universe.

My 'visions' also look back to the 1845 painting by Joseph Severn of Shelley composing *Prometheus Unbound* in the Baths of Caracalla in Rome in early 1819, in which he is sitting in a historical setting with his mind elsewhere, seeing something "otherwise than by ordinary sight", setting down an imaginative vision.

In *Visions of England* I show an England that is a green and pleasant land as in Blake's 'Jerusalem' but has its own culture within European culture. And the last two poems of this selection, written in December 1998 and May 1999, anticipate feelings that the UK faced being fragmented and might need an English Liberation Front, the discontented outlook that led to the vote for Brexit in 2016. In 1991, in *The Fire and the Stones*, I had prophesied that the European Community would become an integrated United States of Europe, which the EU's European Commission now want to create, and several of the poems in this selection can now be seen to have been prophetic in anticipating Brexit and to accord with the current English mood of independence.

Since 1999 I have had all 34 of my poetic volumes published – *Collected Poems* 1958–2005 (1,478 poems, 2006) contained the first 30 volumes, and volumes 31–34 appeared in *Life Cycle and Other New Poems* 2006–2016 (206 new poems, 2016) – along with *Classical Odes* (318 poems, 2006), a total of 2,002 poems in all; and I have written a second epic poem *Armageddon* (2010) about the War on Terror (9/11, Iraq and Afghanistan, 25,000 lines of blank verse). I have also had three more verse plays published. Now, looking back on the poems in *Visions of England* I am struck by their vividness and vitality.

When they appeared in *Collected Poems: A White Radiance*, in *Collected Poems* 1958–2005 and in *Classical Odes* – the last four poems in this selection are classical odes – they were accompanied by sometimes extensive notes, and readers who want to know more about poems such as 'Beauty and Angelhood' can consult these. Withholding the notes emphasises the involvement of the spirit and its visions, intensifies the poems' spiritual focus and brings out their vividness and the vitality of their rhythms. In a few instances – following Ricks' advice in 1979 that I should amend like Tennyson – I have made minor amendments to the original versions of poems.

When I was discovering myself as a poet in Japan while writing 'The Silence', I was accompanied during my afternoon walks in the hot sun by my shadow, a constant companion that became an image for the future wise self I hoped I was heading towards and (in my mind then) would become in my old age. Now, at 78, looking back from the wisdom of my Shadow which I believe I have become, I marvel that Providence, in its wisdom, left me sufficiently clear of public duties to have time to write my works. I cannot help feeling that I did well to spend long hours writing at my desk with (wherever I was living) an inspiring view of my garden, a corner of the universe whose seasonal growth and decay nourished my soul with its vitality just as rustic surroundings nourished the souls of Nature hermits – and Marvell – in bygone times.

The picture of me on the front cover, taken without my knowledge on 14 April 1986, shows me sitting near the cottage believed to have been the "dwelling" of Wordsworth's Solitary, Blea Tarn House between Little Langdale and Great Langdale in England's Lake District, and opening to an imaginative vision that would become 'At Blea Tarn House' (15–16 April 1986, not in this selection) and 'At Cartmel Priory: Taming the Unicorn' (written on 18 April 1986, in this selection). It is a modern equivalent of Severn's picture of Shelley writing in the Baths of Caracalla in Rome (see p.xxiii), and my eyes, too, are in imaginative vision within an inspiring landscape.

15–16, 21, 24, 26, 31 January, 1–3, 5 February 2018

Joseph Severn's 1845 painting of Shelley composing
Prometheus Unbound in the Baths of Caracalla, Rome, in early 1819

Visions of England

The Lone Sailsman in Exile

The friendless foam follows my boat. Island
Mists float and weep. No more is the Kingdom for me,
Only the grate and boom and the wind's bite.
I do not know where I go, whence I come.
The sail shines to the moon, and I must share
Salt on eyes and a heavy chest. I talk
To no-one. Wet, cold, I head for the ice-floes,
The curse of my father's will seething the foam
Behind me as the gull swoops. Empty space
Awaits, when the dark cliff looms from my sleep.

Song of Three Thames-Daughters

"Order *has* been restored,
We have reconstructed our broken land
And buried our ruined continuity
Under new estates and new towns;
The centre is now repaired,
Some other mouth may be as fair as ours
But a crashing blast now brings
Barely remembered frowns."

"We can make our land more just,
Sequestrate the estates of Dukes;   10
Otherwise we have no social purpose
But to maintain the *status quo*.
Washington is the new Rome,
And New Britain, at last alone,
A Hellenistic rally into Europe,
Like an old lady dying
In her rich son's home."

"Ours is the vicarious generation;

Neither lost nor tragic, no longer angry,
We live at one remove   20
Like a bedridden old lady,
Watch others discuss our fate,
Read of others' exploits and decisions
Or lose ourselves in television heroisms,
Courting a garish world,
Unnourished by its synthetic opiate."

ALL:
  "As good a time as any
  To find our way back to the spring
  Of real consciousness within."

An Inner Home

"The forest which surrounds them is their godhead."
(From a review by Mr Geoffrey Gorer of *Wayward Servants*,
a book on the Mbuti pygmies in the Ituri rain forest, N.E. Congo.)

I have followed the Waltham stream:
Winding through sunny meadows,
Stilled by lilies and reeds
It seems a long way from
King Harold's rough-hewn bridge
And Edward's two arches,
Till under the Abbey's tower
On either side of stone
Under two modern humped bridges
With a sudden tugging of weed   10
The stillness overflows
To plunge in a cascade down
And froth into gentle channels
And trickle underground
And I turned away in a panic,

There was weed in my hair and toes.

That child, who, sick from fleeing a baying form,
Lay on the humming Stubbles near the Witches' Copse
Like a sacrificial victim near Stonehenge,
And, seeing a six-spot burnet, suddenly felt secure,   20
Walled round and alone in a forest enclosure;
That child seemed a long way from that adolescent
Who, sick at having seen the universe
In a string of bubbles blown through a child's wire-ring,
Stood in Loughton Camp among writhing pollards
Like nerve tracts rising to a memory rooted in
The skulls of Boadicea's unconscious dead,
And, under the dark grey cortex, distinctly heard
The silence beneath the distant hum of cars
And knew himself under the patter of falling leaves;
And that young man, who, retching at one last sigh,   30
Stood where he fished as a child with sewn flour-bags
And skidded to the island on an icy slide
And stared past his reflection in the gravel pit
As if seeking an image in an unconscious mind,
Until his darkness split, and in the autumn sun
The pond blazed in an unknowable revelation,
He said Yes, and, looking back through the blinding leaves,
He longed to be a statue between the two ponds
And gaze for ever on the thrusting of those trees;
Or that poet, who, sick with impending exile,   40
Having driven round Lippitt's Hill to Tennyson's estate,
Crunched broken glass in the littered Witches' Copse
Alone in the centre of a living *mandala*,
And knew, although before him was approaching stone,
Like a hermit enfolded in a godhead he projects
He would always be enfolded in this Forest,
In this unchangeable image of an inner home.

Like the tree-enfolded face a still stream reflects

Below humped bridges where waving weed is pressed
Before it plunges down and is lost in foam.   50

Orpheus-Philoctetes at High Beach

The leaves turn red, around High Beach
Are beechnuts, toadstools; in Turpin's Cave
The coal fire glows faces, in the grave
Of my love dark phantoms screech.

I twine long hair round a tree nymph's breast,
In a dark glade whisper "Greensleeves!"
And clasp *her* on these fallen leaves,
Shed tears, a highwayman obsessed.

She sits up with leaves in her hair, the moon
Is caught in a forked bare beech tree.
Back at the house my little sleeps peacefully.
Tied to the big clock-tower is a yellow balloon.

I tuck her closer, stroke her hair.
Tomorrow we'll go to Robin Hood Hill
Where oyster mushrooms cling to logs, and she will
Show me her red-veined leaf from the garden pear.

Orpheus-Prometheus in the Blackweir Region of Hell

We looked in this Blackweir pond at sticklebacks
And minnows with green and silver bellies,
At water beetle, skimming dragonflies –
Looked down through the bars, and then picked blackberries.

As a boy I climbed into the round tunnel,
Crouched underground, under this high-barred grate

Where the pond overflows in a cascade down,
Heard voices echoing up to this dungeon gate.

Now squatting beneath the bars within my mind,
Watching gnats dance from an awful torture cell,
I look up at blue sky from a dark tunnel.
Will there ever be an opening in the Gates of Hell?

Flow: Moon and Sea

I loved you like the tortoise-shell
You loved up on the Downs with me.
The light leaps off your Worthing sea
Like shoals of leaping mackerel.

The sea flows like a bent hawthorn.
Now, up the night, the harvest moon
Floats and sails like a child's balloon
Over this darkly rippled corn.

This glow behind the moon and sea
Affects my way of seeing.
What, oh what is happening to my being?
I thrill to a pebble's flow, and a bumble-bee.

Shooting

This weekend my daughter is shooting with Sir John.

I stroll on Staples Hill, where golden leaves and a knighthood
Like moss have buried the footprints of Sir John's grandfather
Who, a hundred years ago, as lord of the manor,
Fenced in a thousand acres of foresters' firewood.

Here brave Willingale lopped a branch
And went to jail.
An Act of Parliament gave these trees back to me,
Sir John's grandfather gave us Lopping Hall, and drew a veil.

My father bought our childhood house from Sir John
Who then left this manor for Lincolnshire.
And now my daughter shoots with him,
Retrieves his pheasants; he gives her antique furniture.

Oh, like a beechwood, levelling down!
May Parliament condemn
All stealers of all trees on Forest hills
And all who flatter them,
And all bringers of revolutionary bills
Who would drag this manorial freedom down –
Let us celebrate all virtuous men.

I have a bone to pick with you, Sir John,
But I will let you keep it. In return,
Teach my daughter your leisured wisdom,
Teach her the good things that the landed learn.

From 'The Flight'
1. A Green Country

Apples are green under a fluttering flag,
Green are my daughter's eyes, green is her breath.
Green are the children among brambles and ferns,
"Oi-olly-ocky," they yodel, "I see Liz,"
Stealing on tiptoe like scrumping thieves.
And let us run together now, across the road, down the hill
    to the Forest,
To where the stream trickles from the long arched tunnel,
And, legs astride it, hands on the curved walls, walk

bow-legged
And stand under the grating overflow, as if in a Hellish
    dungeon.
I took you there, and found a Victorian penny.   10
O this Blackweir pool, where I fished up green frogs in
    flour-bag nets!
We scuffled up through leaves, leaving the water-boatmen and
    dragonflies,
And at a meeting of green paths plunged right, into beeches,
I held your hand and said, "Look, the banks,"
And we ran on back into blackbirds and sticklebacks and newts,
And there, still under water-lilies, was the pond I had not found
    for two decades,
The Lost Pond!

     Apples, pears, wasps.
I came from the Essex flats, green fields round beech thickets.
When the daisies were humming with bees, I lay under
    summer skies.   20
I see a clearing where I kicked a ball, where my father swung
    his lame leg
And scored with a toe-punt. There I picnicked with two boys
    from the first form.
I ran through the Forest in the summers.
I caught caddice in the ponds, I had a glass aquarium that
    cracked at the top,
And green slime slopped down the sides. Near a fallen apple
    tree
I grew tall to the trembling of leaves. Upstairs, under green
    eaves,
I sniffed my death. I said to my brother
"I will live to be a hundred," clicking and reshutting the small
    black cupboard door
Until a voice from downstairs called "Go to sleep."

Brown is the earth of this Clay Country, and hard

under frost,   30
Hard are the fields around Chigwell where we were sent
    on walks,
Stepping over iced hoof-marks in the frozen mud,
O those glistening stiles and brown dark thorns!
Crisp are the leaves of the heart in winter
When the bonfires smoulder no more. Bright is the air,
Remote the golden suns smashed across the icy pool of the sky.
Fingers are numb, cheeks pink, breath misty, clear.

I and my grandfather walked for tobacco in fog,
He fell and blood streamed from his white hair.
He had a stub of a finger he lost in a Canadian saw-mill.   40
Later my father took me for a walk. As we left the gate
The siren wailed. We wheeled to a white white flash,
The whole street shook, the windows clattering out.
Five bombs had fallen. Two houses up the road were
    annihilated
And the cricket field had a hole in it. The war –
I lay in a Morrison shelter and read books, swapped foreign
    notes,
While in the blue air puffs of smoke ended pilots.
When I moved home, I carried my battleship.

Red bricks and lilacs droop over the wooden shed.
On our rockeries, young hearts have wept and bled.   50
Ivy, and a garden hose.
A home is a rattling front door,
A broken flowerpot under a scarlet rose.

Green are the clumps of Warren Hill, green and scummy pond,
Green are the Oaklands fields, green round buttercups,
Green are those fields where children squat in camps,
Green is the ride down Nursery Road, purple the thistles,
Green are the Stubbles and the open heath,
Green is Robin Hood Lane, green past Strawberry Hill,

Green and brown are the two gravel-pit ponds,   60
Green is High Beach, green around Turpin's Cave where
     beechburrs cling to hair,
Green round Lippitt's Hill and the Owl, green the fields beyond,
Green back through Boadicea's camp, where you climbed the
     brown mud walls,
Brown are the leaves round the hollow tree we climbed,
Green along Staples Hill, where we shuffled through leaves to
     the brown stream,
Green past the Wheatsheaf, green up to Baldwin's Hill
Where we ran down to Monk Wood, and you were remote
     from me;
Green holly, green beech leaves, green oaks, and only the trunks
     and banks are brown.
Green to the Wake Arms, green to the Epping Bell,
Green down Ivy Chimneys, green up Flux's Lane   70
Between the poplars and the farmers' fields
Green are the trees round distant Coopersale Hall,
Green are the fields of Abridge and Chigwell,
Green is Roding Valley before hilly Debden,
Green fields, wide open, back into cratered Loughton,
A green country with hosannah-ing pollards, arms raised in
     jubilation.
And green is that gate, green the lime trees that hide the green
     porch door,
Green is that house of echoes. O how you despised my cradle!
You found the buildings false, the people mean and ugly,
But couldn't you feel the kiss in the swishing wind?   80

O the medieval churches of rural Essex:
Magdelen Laver, Abbess Roding, Great Canfield
With its 1250 fresco of Mary offering her breast;
A flat country of fields of wheat and rape
And Elizabethan barns and sleepy hamlets,
3 Lavers, 8 Rodings and 2 Easters.
O Essex, I love your green and drowsy haunts!

All this we have known in the green time, and more.
These are the places I return to now, in my heart-sorrow,
These Essex flats. Here I stood, waiting to meet you,   90
Here I knew you, in a green glade among beechnuts.
Here the city is a boot among yellow lilies, an iron roof that
    blocks the sun.
All this I left for the city, with a young man's impatience;
All this I left, seeking to meet a loyal woman.

I have starlings under my sunflowers.
I love the trunks of these pear-trees, whose ant-bands are sticky.
O these images that haunt me, that I fly to, to which I cling!

Cold Men, A Cold Sky

I drove out one fine Saturday to see the winter.
A hundred miles north of London,
The first patches of frost,
The ice in hoofmarks.
Forlorn crows on ploughed fields frozen white,
Pheasants hugging the road.
I saw iron men striding over white hills
Linked like mountaineers.
Under their heels, flocks of sparrows
Scattered into the hedgerows.
While above, laced with blossom,
The hawthorns wore a grief of snow.
White roofs of farms – all Nature huddled
Against cold climbing giants and a foundry sky.

But oh the warmth of the children in the school hall
Laughing and singing under the Christmas decorations!

Yew

Marble steps, birds' cries, dripping trees,
A seat on a riverside lawn, looking through
Ornamental urns at bare ploughed fields.
Above the splashing weir, hear

                the stillness

                      above the cuckoo.

This is the England I would have as home.
Here is perfect peace, away from crisis crowds. With this view
Here all summer I could ponder like a willow
Or love the earth like that rooted yew.

Rewarded by the Conqueror, D'Abernon
Had this. Where is my reward? MY due?
The city speaks of you with tongues like bells
But here my heart speaks true.

Knight

I go to find the black Knight in this locked country.
The sundial by the river says
"*Sit Patriae Aurea Qua Vis* 1940."

The flint church is unlocked. En-
-ter, roll back the chancel carpet – and stiffen:
Hood, hauberk, sword and shield. 1277.

I have wanted to take a rubbing
Of a gold standard for our time.
I have not found a better model
Than this brass Gawain's reverent mime.

I come out, the sun goes in –

Where is our country's gold?
I will remember the hidden Knight with the steeple hands
In this locked, silent cold.

At Battle: A Violent Event, Serene Nature

Primrose and daffodil scent the hill
Where Harold faced the Norman thrust.
Primrose and crocus where the blood
Of England's flower stained the dust.

Now a great tit see-saws in the thorn,
Sheep graze down to the sparkling lake
And all nature, this serene morning,
Sleeps out its remembrance of a violent ache.

I know a battle a mood from here –
May crocus bloom on that terrain.
May the primrose dance across the fields
That grow over that scarred plain.

Closed

Here I came for my first honeymoon.
The Castle was like my reason.
I wandered round, it was logical –
It is closed now. Winter season.

Across the road in a sloping house
We saw a collection of masks,
Witchdoctor's garb, primitive spears –
Now it is a tea-room. Thermos flasks.

Down by the river we sat on the grass

And looked at summer swans.
Now it is a concrete car park
For minis and pantechnicons.

Only the Norfolk Arms Hotel
Where we spent our wedding night
Remains unclosed. Under the arch I peer for brass.
I cannot remember the room in this sunlight.

I am a lover of tradition
And store castles in my heart.
O may developers never change
This Hotel, this old yellow cart.

Silent Pool

In the woods near Shere
Not far from Newlands Corner
A spring trickles out from a rooted hill
Near pussy willow in the water.

It is limpid clear, the Silent Pool,
All quiet save for piping robins
And warbling children's laughter
Until, beyond the hazel catkins,

It runs into a clear brook,
And tugging mossy weed,
It pours under the path and down a shoot
And cascades into a pond like pigs' feed.

O in my mind there is a spring
And a silent pool below,
Before the froth and the roadside scum
And the chickweed grate and overflow.

Chased

I stand in Shere church
Before the North Wall squint and quatrefoil,
Where Christine Carpenter, anchoress,
Was walled within a hole, like a gargoyle.

I look at ancient petitions.
She broke out and wandered the world,
Was bitten by "the rapacious wolf "
(Satan), anchoress skirts unfurled.

O Christine, you were self-divided.
You wanted to be chaste and chased.
But how unfair that you were judged
By married men who never faced

Your vow, who forced you to keep
What you freely offered one year,
And then freely took back. Walled in
Again, you genuflect despair.

Arundel

Across the river on a hill
The Castle hangs above the town,
Isolated. The ruling class
Shut out the people, kept it down.

Fantail doves cling to the keep walls
Which tower above with battlements.
I cross the drawbridge, mount the steps
And peer at meadows, hear past laments.

I amble through the luxurious rooms.

Old Masters – Howards – line the walls,
Including the Earl of Surrey, who
Invented blank verse, cared where stress falls.

I pass a shield Surrey was given
In Florence. I pass a buffalo's horns.
Then I go to the Fitzalan chapel
Across new-mown lawns.

A wooden Christ on a decaying cross,
Gargoyles, marble tombs – bare flagstones.
One tomb has a statue of a dead man
With a skull and decaying bones.

And this is the truth. A ruling power
Walled round with luxuries must decay.
The people prosper then, but like
An old flag, standards go the same way.

I walk between chestnuts to the gate
And leave this civilised rampart
And have a cream tea in what used
To be the Museum of Primitive Art.

Here when African masks lined the wall
The self was not curbed or restrained.
In our social life and religion
The self should be disciplined, and trained.

I think of Surrey's pentameters,
And the ornate shield in the sumptuous room,
I think of the standards before all freedoms,
The statues on each Fitzalan's tomb,

And I taste the centrist's dilemma:
The bubble round the ruling class

Has been burst by huffing from the left,
Yet standards, like a well-blown glass,

May be huffed to bursting too. On the hill
The Castle hangs above the town
Isolated. The ruling class
Shut out the people, who would level standards down.

At Stoke D'Abernon

At Stoke D'Abernon, in the old Manor
House whose veranda overlooks the country river,
Fifty Heads of English weekend on the latest methods.
"English should be integrated," some say like demigods,
And, "Teach fiction for its social content," or, "Forget their
    tense,
Let them express themselves, mark them as an audience.
We cannot *judge* them, after all. Why should their work be
    checked,
If they write 'we was', it's their dialect."
The old values have been dammed; curling over the weir
A great confusion froths beyond the Saxon church, like a
    slovenly prayer.   10

There is a belief in the goodness of the human will,
The Pelagian heresy is with us. This mindless caryatid is still
A classroom lout? "Perfect at fifteen, with no more to learn.
Forget that he is a pillar, his *response* is our concern.
'Knowledge' and books are outside him. Daunting.
Bracket them out, let him *express* his self-flaunting.
It is the Age, the Individual reigns,
Born free with Rousseau, in educational chains,
He must be treated like colonial soil."
('A perfect State' – surrender of empire. And Arab oil.)   20

⌐The church bells toll, I leave the waterfall for the graveyard.
Among these Norman arches I am under a standard.
Here all can know imperfection, their 'original sin',
Here they can bow to literacy through the stained glass Anne.
Here they can break out of their church-door hearts into
    ploughed fields where
Like winds, they can merge with the currents of the years. Here
They can connect themselves to seven hundred years of tombs
Flung up from the Flow through great men's drawing-rooms
Now strewn round this chantry like *débris* from a surging river,
These monuments to energies we remember.   30

I measure my shadow before the altar
Against this Augustinian Knight in the chancel floor.
This brass 'should' of centuries shames our 'want',
Those still fingers steeple the discipline of the font
And of the quiet respect for law that keeps streets free.
Some said, "We should boycott this class-conscious exam." 'We',
Like unions battering laws of governments –
In schools, politics and marriage, there is a turbulence,
The rushing freedom of the play of light on foaming shallows.
How can children find their way back to the deeps if the
    teachers become their shadows?   40

The dam has raised the river's level, here by this garden urn
It irrigates the ploughed fields. Here a line is drawn
Across the riverbed of our minds. Let us walk back to where
The currents from upstream float serenely through – and stare
On Western man: the selfless Knight, the perverse, Romantic
    will.
Let us open ourselves to this tugging under the surface. Eyes
    closed, and still,
Let us empty our splashing hearts and see through the mirrored
    morning
Where one point of light breaks like a sun. Darkened round
    that dawning,

By this garden urn I know: this still, floating surface measures
    my search –
The God in my days and centuries, by the Saxon standard of
    that little church.   50

Tattershall Castle

"An Englishman's Home is his Castle"

A tall red brick tower from the outer moat.
Peacocks dance where the guard-house snowdrops float
On sky. We cross to the inner ward – we have an hour –
And walk to the *'donjon'*, to the great tower,
Climb steps to the brickwork guard room, and exclaim
At the ancient fireplace, where coats of arms proclaim
Baron Cromwell's emblem, like a housewife's purse,
And motto: *'N'ay je droit?'* Do I not have the right?
                      An arrogant verse.

A high-rise palace, also fortified.
The winding turret stair shines with the polished stride   10
Of soldiers. A great hall with fireplace – we climb
On to Lord Cromwell's chamber for withdrawing time.
Up, up; we pass the women's hall, and talk
Our way up to the turreted roof, the parapet walk.
Below the battlements, green fields that have not risen;
I am an unpopular Treasurer in an enemy-free time –
    is this not a prison?

My daughter says, "Look, I live over there." I deprecate
Those small quarters, that squat modern estate.
I wore a purse once – did *I* not have the right to protect?
That theft is beneath me, like the stair to this prospect.   20
My daughter drops a stone from a decade down, my next wife
Presses my hand. In a towering dungeon I spent my life.

But then I think: a home is like the mind,
And can I not live on many floors, in a variety of chambers,
   like the wind?

This is a permanent place: from well to battlement
This moated home stands for a fortified marriage. I relent
And glance at the woman I will wed within a week, and tell
Myself: we shall be apart from the world, drawing from our well,
Warm in our halls by our hearth, under stained glass knights;
We will climb the mind's stairs to its turreted heights,   30
Then descend to the third floor spandrel, and quietly trace
Our gromwell weed on our hand-carved fireplace.

This stone *'agger'* withstood the Carolines, will soon hear
A new voice laughing down the echoing stair.
Outside my daughter picks snowdrops by the moat,
My next wife watches a peacock, whose hidden eyes denote
An artist. By a garden roller I renew my choice;
From the Bede House hedge I look back and rejoice
For the *'donjon'* has come through. Having survived the gale,
Let the peacock jump and fan its eyebright tail!   40

High Beach Church

Hoofs clop clop clop between the silver birch
Along the road beside this forest church.
Come through the omega lych-gate, down the steps by the yew,
Hear where the bracken tangles and wood-pigeons coo.
On this green carpet pause; an evening nightingale
Sings through Eternity. Here I will be buried by this black rail.
A crocus blooms where every heart believes
That unknown faces mean more than autumn leaves.

The aisle is quiet, I tiptoe to the chancel.
Altar, pulpit, stained glass, hammerbeam, and a lectern eagle.   10

A hundred years of scullery floors; for sixty-seven
The local schoolmaster played that organ.
Here on the wall two marble tablets state
The Ten Commandments, and how to meditate.
Red and black, a life like scullery tiles;
Where the robin hops, a wife is wreathed in smiles.

'No graven images', 'no other gods but me',
No murder, do not covet; no adultery.
I think of a host who wanted – and too fast –
What now I give to manna, and to last.   20
Unlike London, where a smile is like a pillow,
Here girls are like a shower of pussy willow.
This is a rooted life, like the evergreen yew.
No glass or redbrick spoils this woodland pew.

Let us be faithful to these hillocked dead,
Whether poet, politician or Department Head,
Let our deeds, like bluebells on a mound of moss,
Attest a Britain like a marble cross.
Now like a civil servant, now like a gardener-surgeon
Let us cut the creeping cancer, that the health may burgeon.   30
Let us conserve the diamond lead window standards
From well-meaning revolutionary vanguards.

Silver birch and bracken, and folk who doubtless sinned
All feed the silence under this March wind.
Shh! rest in the Eternal – hear the dragging of a snail
Beneath the water-warbling of the nightingale.
Here rustling moments are threescore muffled thieves
And pale faces under hillocks, like last autumn's leaves,
Are compost for this crocus. Let me leave behind
A meaning like this purple crocus, when I am blind.   40

Death has its beauty: the hearse, a squirrel's tail.
My coffin will be lowered by this black rail,

Between this laurel, this holly. My companions,
Unknown Belshams, Hepburns and Cookes, near the
    rhododendrons.
Like a crocus under sticky buds, I will blink and brim
At the tinkling of the water-finches, and the distant hymn,
Snug under grass, safe from nettles, brambles. And in the rain
I will dream of the arrow on the Victorian weathervane!

Porthleven

A harbour in two hills at dusk. Things of the sea
On the privately owned front. A boatyard, the crab factory,
Nets. Fishing boats on the sand, on the "pier"
The sea smashes and booms. Trailing bladderwrack. Here
Is a living from the sea. Unlike Mevagissey
It is not commercialised, it is very much a community.
Once a year they sing "For those in Peril"
While a church and anchor light up on the bare hill.

Five churches, two pubs. A cross, a lighthouse, a boat are
    what yields
A simple life. Round here there are dolmens in fields,   10
I once did a tour of them on a bicycle from Marazion.
Tin-mine chimneys and ivied arches stand on
Moors. Stone walls and hedges, orange bugle lilies. Neighbours
Walk into our in-laws' parlour, recite the labours
Of giants, or the *Triptania* wreck on Loe Bar,
And offer mackerel bait for the fishing jar.

The Harbour Hotel shows 'Porthleven
1750'. It was a cove and a few cottages then.
A cemetery up on one hill. On every chimney-pot
Gulls scream, like souls of the dead defending what   20
Their living own. History and death.... Tonight we stay
For it is the village's annual march round the fairy-lit bay.

Now they come, behind the band, each holding an orange torch.
    We admire
The sight until they throw their lighted brands on a great
    bonfire.

Red sparks in the night. White stars. Village faces.
Here is the unity of men against rocky places.
Now in this inner harbour, on the Clock Tower side,
The Divine Spirit approaches like a creeping tide.
I think of how a view across St Ives' night-lit bay
Inspired a vision of Christ and the Mystic Way.   30
My wife has brought me back to this. Yet I would miss
    the stimulation
Of the centre if I lived here, there would be suffocation.

We will visit this corner of England every year, perhaps even
    retire
Here. And perhaps the Gorran haven will again inspire
The heart that chose exile at Portmellon. Here in the simple
    life
Men live against the weather, the sea, the wife,
Go to the cemetery and return as gulls
Wheeling round the rooftop that once sheltered their skulls;
Here men mend nets, then go out, torchlights on the sea,
And trawl the waters of God's teeming plenty.   40

The Royal Observatory, Greenwich

I walk in a drive of chestnuts and conkers, and regard
What Wolfe looks over: a city like a graveyard.
High rise tombstones, smoking crematorial chimneys, and over
The Queen's House and colonnade, the brown river
Where Nelson's coffin embarked. One o'clock. From the top
Of the mast on Flamsteed's House, watch the large time ball drop,
A public measurement of time for Victorian

Shipping, above the cobbled gutter of the Prime Meridian.

Greenwich! Here I did penance in a ragged school,
And met my second wife. The river, this park rule   10
That stretch in Hell. I brought vandals to see these sundials
On the wall – zodiac, equal and unequal hours. They were trials,
Those visits. I go up to the Octagon Room where the
First Astronomer Royal tried to measure longitude at sea –
How far East or West mariners sailed – and the Equation of
      Time,
The difference between the clocks and when the stars climb.

I have also measured East and West, the years have left me
      sadder.
Tompion clocks, a telescope through a ladder.
I go downstairs to the equatorial sextants,
The mural quadrants and transit instruments.   20
I come to the Bradley Meridian, and beyond
Is the Mean Time Clock, accurate to a tenth of a second,
And the Airy Transit Circle which points its proof
Like a cannon thundering through an unshuttered roof.

A frosty night, a sweep of glittering dust;
All this bombarding of the universe is so much rust.
Newton needed their figures for his law of gravity
And shut out a sparkle with his scientific curiosity.
Measuring Eternity with gold lines, they cut up
The shadows that flow from the sundial, or the buttercup.   30
They organised their darkness, but missed the sun,
Squinting up a telescope at a black heaven.

Would there were an Observatory for the inner dark!
I would loll in my reclining seat and embark
Into space, breathe deeply, then in the blackest night,
Peer up the telescope for the dawning Light,
Feel the tide of Eternity rush under my heart,

Then, having counted the planetary hours, come to with a start,
Go outside, look at the gold lettering near the clover
Leaf, and see if the clovered shadow has cascaded it over!   40

Loughton Methodist Church

A redbrick chapel behind a low wall.
A cross (once bombed), two turrets, stained glass – all
Spoilt by the olive-green doors. Locked. Round the side we
Peer through coloured glass into a rippling sea.
Through the porch, two aisles, yellow pews, each with a
     cardholder,
Book-ledge and umbrella space. A table altar,
Yellow pulpit, new organ pipes. A smashed pane. I peep and spy
The old hymn board, and the clock I measured sermons by!

I am shut out of where I sat every Sunday
Until our Minister preached against Suez. Next Friday   10
My letter was in the *Gazette*. Here my mother
Brought me. Two of her grandparents were Methodists from
     Yorkshire, and another
Wore a top hat to the chapel at Brixton Hill.
They lived through the second flowering of the Puritan daffodil.
Pink tulips on green glass, a wooden roof.
My father's family were Norsemen and Quakers, though there
     is little proof.

Here a host of characters passed, in fellowship, beyond hell:
Twisted old man Occomore, lean Mr Bedwell.
Here circuit and lay preachers, the latter-day Puritan,
Interpreted the faith in terms of their Wesleyan   20
Hearts – "the Redeeming Blood" – and spontaneous prayer.
Here they made themselves tiny gods, making up their
Rules to suit their belief: application,
Sober living, hard work, thrift, Sabbath observance – nothing

about illumination.

At school I attended Anglican morning song,
Found instruction from repeated prayers that contain strong
Rules, as my mother does now, having changed to the psalter.
In her church, my brother was organist, my daughter
Was in the choir. Wearing a violet cassock, she rang
The bell where my father's coffin stood, we all sang   30
'Hail, gladdening Light'. In that church there is a rule
To which the self is subordinated, like a spirit-school.

We live in darkness, until in quiet the Light
Shines through the soul, and teaches what is right.
Our churches must be places of quiet and candles
Which fill with peace. Like Catholic confessionals,
They must say 'Don't' to the wants of the errant self-will
Which exclude the guiding Spirit and make the soul ill.
They must make us feel it through the heart, not through the
    head.
There must be mysticism, or God is dead.   40

For this the heart must be freed – by Rule. Yet where
To find it? Our religion is overgrown, like a pear
Tree that has never been pruned. Fifteen hundred years,
Then the Anglicans split, then the Puritan tears
On the branches. Noncomformists and Separatists –
From Luther and Calvin, and the Baptists,
Congregationalists, Presbyterians, Quakers on whom the sun
    shines,
Till Methodists and Evangelicals grew new signs.

Where in all this dead wood can the individual begin?
For a blind man to deny the sun is sin.   50
The freewill makes hardened choices until
It softens to guidance to let the Spirit fill
It with calm and Light. All else is confusion.

Our darkened nation needs a sap transfusion.
The priests are gardeners with a calling, who apply the Rule.
They are right to keep us from darkness, and the fool.

Unity is the hope for Quaker men of Light
Who want symbols to prune the darkness for what is right.
All sects must come together. Only then can I again
Listen, in these Rule-less pews, for the silence beneath
   Sunday rain.   60
I wander round the back to the old hall
I acted in when five. Connecting seats. On the wall:
GOD IS WITH US. On either side parked cars press
Where there were fields. The old rural freshness

And simplicity have lost to urbanisation.
On each side a wire fence with a concentration
Camp's barbed wire. Up it, by the new hall,
White bells of bellbind ring down the new brick wall.
I walk back past the tulips to the High Road.
I am shut out of this ground where I was sowed   70
Like a tulip to be choked by bellbind, where I felt the fold
Or their Rule-less notions, like chickweed round a marigold!

Our Lady of Victories

I go out, walk the dank streets of Labour rule
To our polling booth: Our Lady of Victories School.
People saunter. A teller hands me my vote,
I go to the cubicle for this historical footnote.
A pencil hangs from new string. I make my cross,
Slot it into the tin as if a Tory loss
Were in doubt. Outside I feel a cleansing beauty:
It is so proudly futile, this democratic duty.

In February it was a wintery morning.

People wore coats, there was a spring in the step – and
    a warning. 10
Now all seem listless. Politicians
Have quietened their voices, but the same abstractions
And slogans will water our garden. We are like flowers.
We get gardeners whose ideas are not ours.
'To represent'.... The *genus* looks plausible,
But true values bloom, like petals, in the individual.

A crisis is on us. The increased price of oil,
Our fertiliser, will bankrupt us, spoil
Our garden. Our social democracy must harshen.
Hardship will blight Western civilisation. 20
The Golden Age of Churchill is near its finish.
Whoever wins has neither the power nor the wish
To resist the Arabs. Will the UK break up?
After all, our Empire proved as frail as a buttercup.

Night. On the television the first return
Shows a swing to Labour. "This means they will earn
A healthy overall majority."
Behind the curtain crouches a new society.
There will be more clipping and pruning, the State –
To be fair – will cut blooms to pay the new Arab rate. 30
We will be snipped and scythed, roses will squeal:
Wealth tax, gift tax, and a nationalising sickle of steel.

Torn-off leaves to pay for a dust to sprinkle
Round headless levelled stalks – that are now equal!
The *genus* has no flowers. Let us, then, lack
Fertiliser and brackish water, and go back
To blooms and petals, to the family stem,
To the responsible gardener, working, leaving them
Disciplined, well-pruned among vegetables
That will sell. No degenerate stock under old labels. 40

Now sacrifice and revolution are in the air.
Will the People submit to the doctrinaire,
Or will there be anarchy, a *coup*, a dictator's drive?
Will our Parliamentary democracy survive,
This ritual canvassing for the right to rule,
One equal cross for the genius and the fool?
Yet this method of Pericles will tantalise
Long after it has been discontinued as a pack of lies.

An old penny. Britannia! Under your shield
We won victories on many a battlefield: 50
Against Philip of Spain, Napoleon, the Kaiser, Hitler.
Are we to fall from within like Rome? Is it better
For patrician stability to be destroyed
By populist leaders? Help us avoid
A catastrophe in our broken-down civilisation,
O Lady of Victories; help us restore our nation!

Southwark Cathedral

I walk round the Cathedral. At the front
The altar-screen shows statues of saints in niches.
I see the tombs of Gower, and Bishop Andrewes,
The Bunyan window. I revere these cultural riches.

On the fifteenth-century roof there are bosses
With medieval faces, of Gluttony and
Lying and other sins. This place connects me
With past generations, who have banned

The easy, unreal values. I must accept
This ground that guards the illumined silence,
This saintly quiet of the aisle and retrochoir,
Which contains the reality of traditional excellence.

Pilgrims' Pavement
(In Canterbury Cathedral)

From the gardens, the structure impresses me.
It is solid, in proportion, perspective,
Towers balanced in stone; expressed beauty:
All arts built together with one objective –

Architecture, stained glass, sculptures in niches –
To serve God. What energy, what vision!
Inside, I follow the path great Chaucer took
Past the cloister door where the knights rushed their decision

And the base of the wall where Becket fell.
I climb the polished steps to the Trinity Chapel
Where the Shrine of St Thomas stood until
Henry the Eighth destroyed it. There I dwell

On the polished ridge where countless pilgrims kneeled.
The stones in the pavement are worn by revering pairs
Of feet: the zodiac roundels by the mosaic
Of a world in a *mandala* of circled squares.

In each month someone is doing something.
February, warming hands, March digging. Since
April is pruning I lament a tradition
Between the tombs of Henry the Fourth and the Black Prince.

Above the Black Prince is a painting of God
On a rainbow of gold. This is how they
Saw Him, those medievals, controlling
The universe. And they were right! Today

How wrong we are, with our science, our rockets
To the moon, what our glassy architecture has cost!
Let us preserve this pavement of the past

As a living symbol of all that we have lost.

A Thought for Winter
The Fertile Soil of Nature: January to June
(From 'The Weed-Garden')

O how souls would grow if they used their eyes
And ears on the *flora* and *fauna*, the butterflies,
Birds, animals, flowers, hedgerows, trees and seas
That nourish throughout the year! See hive bees
Swarm in January, the male yew flowers, a mistle-
Thrush and – hear – a great tit call near a thistle.
Gorse flames, ash twigs are in bud, and plu-plu-plu   410
Plu-plu-plu, sings a green woodpecker. Through
Honeysuckle buds, see, woodbine, blackthorn.
Coltsfoot hangs its head now it rains, trout spawn;
See the footprints of the water vole under ivy
Fruit, hear the vixen scream, the dog-fox yelp in the early
Dark. Now a brimstone flutters near elm and alder
Flower, and hazel catkins, and the yellowhammer
Chirps, "A little bit of bread and no cheese."
See footprints of squirrel and stoat. Red toadstools squeeze
Through near the barren strawberry. Jackdaws flap   420
Round the church tower, blue tits chase, twitter and scrap.
Wrens search for spiders. Now, from winter sleep
In rafters, Red Admirals and peacocks peep,
And small tortoiseshells. Sticky horse chestnut buds
Unfold in the sunshine, a great white cloud scuds
Over blue. A squirrel and a wood pigeon feed
On fresh green leaves. See, thrushes and blackbirds speed
North. Wheatears and chiffchaffs flit. A chaffinch sings
From telegraph wires, a white bar on its wings.
Violets, sallow, and a hare. Marsh marigold   430
Blaze near some toadspawn, a necklace of cold
Eggs. See: a mole, a shrew, and a sleepy hedgehog.

Now it is primrose time. By this Forest log,
Crab apple and guelder rose. Shh! a heron, in that copse.
See ravens on those crags, crossbills in the fir tree tops.
Now all Nature is awake. Cowslips, bluebells.
Oak, beech, walnut put out last leaves, and smells.
Willow catkins are out. Horse-tails. An orange tip,
A small copper, a holly blue, all skip
By a seven-spot ladybird eating greenflies   440
On a leaf. Newt eggs on pond weed, and in the skies,
Swallows, house-martins return, and the cuckoo.
See willow-warblers, blackcaps, nightingales through
Leaves, see nests of thrush and blackbird, and in high
Thorn, the domed nest of twigs of a magpie.
Now is the month of flowering trees and plants.
All is fresh and bright and green, the beech woods dance.
There are orchids in the meadow, and white hawthorn,
White candles on horse chestnut, bats above the lawn.
See, a blue tit is eating a caterpillar up,   450
While mayflies gad round a water buttercup.
Dandelions by a wasp's nest, fairy ring
Toadstools. Swifts scream and circle in the fine evening.
The hen-pheasant sits, the water forget-me-not
Blinks yellow eyes. In the birch and bracken a spot-
-ted flycatcher, a nightjar. A wealth of song!
Linnets, goldcrests, tits clamour all day long
For food. Young robins. Now the scent of new-
Cut hay being cocked and carted disturbs two
Rabbits. Weasels, rats, hedgehogs, partridges, stoats,   460
Owls fly for mice there, voles search near river boats
For young. Here pick woodruff and smell new-mown
Grass in winter. In field and wood, on ston-
-y moor and heath, by mountain and waterside:
Butterflies. White admirals, large blues glide,
Fritillaries, ringlets. Caterpillars teem,
Tortoiseshells' on stinging-nettles, lime-hawks' gleam
On lime trees. Birds have bedraggled feathers,

As they approach the moult. In certain weathers
See swallow skim, see the vermilion hind wing 470
Of a cinnabar moth near ragwort, fluttering
On the downs, or lacewing near the field rose.
Black slugs. A snail eats leaves near a garden hose,
Gnats and midges dance over the water butt,
The foliage teems with grubs round the summer-hut,
The garden is full of crawling, hopping pests.
Humble-bees in the foxgloves, a honey-bee quests
In the dead nettles. Scarlet poppies in the corn-
-fields, boletus in the woods, the newly born
Bullhead fish – "miller's thumb" – dart in the pond, 480
Near ferns: moonwort and adder's tongue. Beyond
Yellow water-lilies, red deer and badgers' earths.
The seashore is strewn with starfish and afterbirths:
Jellies, seaweed. Bladderwrack, Irish moss,
Green laver. Sand sedge, sea rocket, hound's tongue toss
In the wind. In the rocks limpets, whelks cling to a slab
Near a strawberry anemone, and a hermit crab.

At Roche Chapel

From the road, massive jagged rocks appear among
Bracken, with a tower built on top of the high-
-est – an arch; the ruined chapel. I cross and climb.
Above me towers the chapel of St Mi-

-chael; a local hermit who lived a hundred feet
Up there, perched in a precarious eagle's nest.
I climb the path, scale an iron ladder in-
-to the chapel, another to the cell. I rest.

Below me, spread out against the sky, the fields
And hills of Cornwall to the china clay
Mounds. I perch here, high above the world's desires,

Living to praise God's creation and pray

For the people below who put bread in
My lowered rope-basket. I am above
Temptation, lifted Godwards to the sky,
In the terrain of the kestrel, a peaceful dove.

Lightning over Polruan

Near the ivy house where Q annotated
For fifty-two years, in Fowey, we first park,
Then chug-chug in the ferry across silver ripples
Among boat-masts into the gathering dark.

Dusk and lights. The wizened white-haired ferryman
Takes the silver obol from my tongue as we ply.
A dozen crabs scuttled by the jetty, but now
The water is a surface, under a cloudy sky.

He helps us off on to the steps of the pier.
We climb into Polruan, an underworld   10
Of tiny streets, houses without curtains,
Lights and open front doors, where events have swirled

With the tides. "For Sale": a cottage, one up one down.
And should we settle here and gaze across the creek
And live out the rest of Eternity in this
Backwater, a Sunday every day of the week?

Lightning flickers over Polruan hill
Like lights turned on and off in an attic.
Distant thunder rumbles. It is nearly dark.
Lights gleam round Fowey. Must the past last in the quick?   20

"Let's go back," I say, remembering what to forget,

Wanting to return to the present. We climb
Down and arrive at the landing-jetty as
The ferry-boat chugs back another time.

From the Stygian water the dark sky
Is lit with flickering yellow fire. "Go
Back home quick before the thunder comes," says
The old ferryman, crouching near his mo-

-tor. Safely ashore we hurry to the car park.
Our visit to Hell is past, our escape complete.   30
One day I may, like Q, write here, over boats.
Until then I will live in Paradise Street.

Trenarren

It is raining this afternoon, so we will drive
Along the cliffs to the road for Trenarren.
We will turn down the lane and park at the end,
And walk down the track between hedges, and then

We will saunter a mile between high hedgerows
That are filled with every kind of August flower:
Sheep's-bit scabious, ragwort, woodruff, cuckoo-pint.
The leaves meet over our heads, protect us from the shower.

Now we come out on to the damp headland.
The way lies open now, to the Black Head.
We cross a rocky field, and far below
The sea foams on brown rocks, a deserted

Cove. O, my love, when I have at last passed on,
You will find me flitting as a dragonfly
Across my Forest pond, or here as a gull,
Wheeling down over Trenarren, soaring by!

Arthur's Innocence

We take the Land Rover down the parish track
And climb the steep hill to the old castle,
The inner ward. I look at the island fort,
The sea below, this rocky Tintagel!

Here Merlin took Arthur down the cliff path
To that cave below on the pebbled beach.
Here chess-playing Tristram brought his Iseult
To marry Mark, and lived out of his reach.

The caves of the world hide many children
Who have left their two parents' care. Ah well,
Guinevere had yet to love Sir Launcelot and
Arthur did not know she would share Iseult's married Hell.

Ghost Town

I walked in a valley in the heart of London.
I stood in a potato field and saw the yellow
Mining town which had been deserted. There were
Narrow streets of low houses, each window

Was shuttered. As I squeezed between the walls
Of this ghost town, I saw trousered legs un-
-der the half-open shutters, and heads back still.
Men sat in the windows. Could these be the dead whom no-one

Would take in the exodus? I peered up at the face
Of one. It was an old man's, well shaven and pale.
But oh the horror as his closed eye opened
And peeped out of its corner, the awful detail!

Shuddering, shivering, I walked past the living dead,

Sitting motionless, they opened their eyes and peep-
-ed. How relieved I was to come out in the valley.
Nothing would make me return to where those dead sleep.

Energy Techniques

Living in a time of falling standards,
We think we are slithering down, like Rome before the Goths.
Will oil save us, or will it break up the UK,
Or, because we've borrowed against it, leave us like slicked moths?

Will it last more than fifty years? Will North Sea
Gas? And what of the coal prices, electricity?
It is with relief that I hear that the future
Is (through silicon) solar, or marine energy.

Energy from the sun, or from the waves
May put out of date our 'aids to living', so clever-
-ly 'harnessed', as the gas lamp, the candle have gone,
And may progress our civilisation for ever!

I think of Norman buildings, and our advance
Since then. Perhaps we will have perpetual progress.
Perpetual progress! It is just a dream.
We have techniques, and there are many more bless-

-ings and discoveries budding in our scientists' minds,
But history is not like a rising line on a graph,
One sales boom. It is a zigzag, and Dark Ages
Make valleys of low blankness, and sunless half-

Bloomed souls. And look at the Norman Cathedrals,
What splendid buildings! By our low slopes, they are peaks
On the up-down mountain-range of civilisation.
Our dreams, lacking *élan*, are of energy techniques.

Wistful Time-Travellers
(First Version)

Sitting here in our flat, after dinner,
We can turn on the past. One TV knob, and Lord-
-s of Time, we are back eight years at the Marathon.
It could be twelve years ago on a tape-record-

-er. Our voices will speak from that Christmas, at a touch
Of a key. Or if I put up a screen, I could be
Me as I was at a wedding fifteen years back
In a garden of celluloid Eternity.

We Westerners are all time-travellers now.
We glide at the speed of light. For a few pounds
We can put back the clock to yesterday,
Fill the present with yesterday's sights and sounds –

Football, cricket, boxing, thrillers, or songs,
Memories on tape or film or a round disc,
Available in the home, or the waves of the air,
To escape the present for a vicarious risk.

We needed the past when we were doddering.
We looked nostalgically back to the Golden noon
When the West held, baffled that the mightiest,
Most inventive civilisation, whose offshoot reached the moon,

Should, after D-Day, shrink in senescent ruin,
Retreat in a world which prefers the tyrant's prime
To our old system. Whispering disapproval,
We Westerners wistfully escape the present time.

A Metaphysical in Marvell's Garden

The House is hidden down lanes of the mind,
It stands "Strictly Private" amid green fields,
Over the redbrick front, a weathercock.
Behind, sunny lawns. Shaped evergreen shields
A huge cedar. And here a long green pond
Winds past the stone arch of a nun's chapel.
A Roman tomb ponders the October,
The ragged roses remember Marvell.

Here shed body like a sheepskin jacket,
Discard all thought as in a mystery school.   10
By this nun's grave sit and be the moment,
A oneness gazing on the heart's green pool.
A universe unfolds between two stone columns
And takes a leafy shape on clouded ground.
The sun-lily floats. Question its waters,
It will trickle through your fingers and be drowned.

The South Front sundial says in coloured glass
"*Qui Est Non Hodie*". I am a bowl.
In the North Hall the piano-tuner
Ping ping pings and trembles through my soul.   20
Who would not live in this delicious quiet,
Walk among columns, lie on the grass and wait?
Who would not teach a Fairfax daughter here,
Escape all bills, be free to contemplate

A flowered soul rooted like a climbing rose,
Metaphysical swoon of gold moments
Whose images curl down through thorns and leaves
(Wit and wordplay), spirit and satin sense;
Petalled layers and folds of whorled meaning
In whose dew-perfumed bowls a divine breeze blows;   30
Or like the prickly flame of the firethorn

Which crackles where purgation merely glows?

With drowsed eyes glance at solid grass and be
In whirlpools of energy like a sea.
Breaths heave the light, and answering currents pour
Through spongy stones and stars, or seaweed tree.
Now see with eye of mind into swelled form,
Imagine sap wash, oak wave in acorn.
Knowers are one with known, and are soaked by tides
That foam and billow through an ebbing lawn.   40

Gaze down on galaxies in a stone bowl
Like curved rose petals (small tip, large end),
Bent, cracked to holes. Travel faster than light
Through wisdom to where many curled worlds bend,
See nightmare multiplicity, then go
Where the bud of each universe is found,
The great Rose-tree of light where grown Ideas
Drift into form as petals fall to ground.

The vision has now passed. Condemned to crowds,
Town seers must teach hordes and leave halls' green waters   50
To lords who never peep for secret flowers
Or climb their souls up walls; and to their daughters,
And now a cloud flits through a fairy ring
And I glimpse for an instant my little "T.C."
And feel a dreadful shudder across my calm,
A "May it not come yet, but wait for me".

Wall-high climbers, whose many blooms reflect
Glimpses of the rose on the great Rose-tree
Which forms all souls in Time from one rose-hip,
Whose past growth glows gold moments they still see,   60
Are, in the present, one essential rose;
Which novices may see as a watery
Dark's shimmer and glimmer of the timeless

Dew-filled bowl of one gold water-lily.

Nymph everywhere, for whom men sacrifice
Paradise for a mortgaged, salaried mask
To keep you where Tennyson longed for Maud
Or where you board, town climbers only ask
That, eyes closed, you grow a golden lily
And be a bowl for it, and simply start   70
To wimple in your wanting. May you be
A rose-sun-leaf-ground-cloudy fire-gold heart.

A Crocus in the Churchyard

Hoofs clop clop clop between the silver birch
That hide the arrowed spire and this Forest church.
Come through the lych-gate, down steps by the yew:
Where the bracken tangles, wood-pigeons coo.
On this green carpet, pause: a nightingale
Sings through eternity by a black rail.
A crocus blooms where every heart believes
That unknown faces mean more than autumn leaves.

The aisle is quiet, tiptoe to the chancel.
Altar, pulpit, stained glass, lectern eagle,   10
Hammerbeam roof, a tiled Victorian floor,
The font and cattle brands, organ by the door.
Here on the wall two marble tablets state
The Ten Commandments, and how to contemplate.
Red and black, a life like scullery tiles;
Where a robin hops, a wife is wreathed in smiles.

"No graven images", "no gods but me",
No murder or covetous adultery.
A time when no host wanted, it would seem,
And manna was not yet a juicy dream.   20

A city smile is like a warm pillow,
Here girls are like a shower of pussy willow.
A rooted life, like the evergreen yew:
No glass or redbrick spoils each woodland pew.

The church is faithful to its hillocked dead.
Whether poet, agent, or Department Head,
Their deeds, like bluebells on a mound of moss,
Attest a Britain like a marble cross.
They, like bent gardeners in their commonwealth,
Cut bellbind and preserved their belief's health,   30
Conserved the diamond lead window standards
From the stones of revolutionary vanguards.

Silver birch, bracken and folk who seldom sinned
Now feed the silence under this March wind.
Shh! rest in the eternal; hear a snail
Dragging beneath the warbling nightingale.
Here rustling moments are time's muffled thieves;
Faces under hillocks, unlike old leaves,
Are compost so a crocus can proclaim:
To glimpse a Golden Flower is man's true aim.   40

Under this hillock, a decaying heart
Feeds the roots of a crocus and takes part
In the lost blowings of time from a windless
Ecstasy's silence and brimming stillness,
And, filled with dews, can, like an art-work, hold
A mirror down to Nature and still gold
Sunshine so posthumous meaning can wave
From fields of silver light beyond the grave.

Under the spire that towers from the slate roof
With arrowhead and vane like rational proof,   50
Look up at a high tripod which can view
White clouds that scud across the darkening blue,

And startle God at His theodolite,
As, measuring the angles of clouds and night,
He takes a reading of time's speed and flow
And calculates the centuries still to go.

Death has its beauty. A hearse, a squirrel's tail,
And your coffin is lowered by this black rail,
Between laurel and holly. For companions,
Unknown Belshams, Cookes, and rhododendrons.   60
A crocus under buds, now blink and brim
At dew-dipping finches, a tinkling hymn,
Snug in grass, safe from brambles; and in fine rain,
Gaze at the still arrow on the windless weathervane.

Pear-Ripening House

A gable behind lime trees, a green gate
Which says "Journey's End". In the porch we wait
By the grained door, then go by pebbledash
Garage and shed which have seen small boys bash
Centuries before lunch against Australia,
Past roses (at square leg), a dahlia,
And a splurge of storm-beaten daisies, for
The old pear tree tumbles by the back door.

Now in this room peep – under four black beams,
Sloping ceilings – for the mirror where gleams   10
The yearning of a reaching out to moons,
Where flit the ghosts of a thousand afternoons.
This, and the black Victorian clock that cowers
Between two prancing horses, measured the hours
Of falling generations, crops of pears,
The sunsets and winters up and down the stairs.

Here floats a battleship on a lino sea;

The day war ended, this was ARP.
Here slides the ghost of a brooding schoolboy,
A fire-warmed clerk reading in lonely joy.   20
Here flits a brief affair, a wedding eve,
Here steals a separation. The shadows grieve.
Families, funerals.... A Parthenon,
This house is permanent, we are the gone.

Now thirty years are less than the straggly twines
That were honeysuckle. And still the sun shines!
Dressing for church is the green of last spring's
Lilac; young ambitions and hankerings
Are now the floatings of a dandelion clock.
What meaning had they? Is Time just the block   30
And blackened stump of a hewn sweet chestnut?
Cascading ivy that drowned a summer-hut?

Young wants and hankerings have a meaning
To the hard-skinned ego's slow mellowing.
The journey through maturing hours and years
Ends in wrinkling pith and pitying tears.
Cores fill with heavy juices from one flow
Whose sap softens to soul the hard ego.
All life ripens to drowse back to the One:
Fruit and old men fall earthward from the sun.   40

Ripe pears return pips to the ground, and sow
A next life's genes, patterned on this one. Know
That soul inherits genes from its last spring now
To gush a vision of buds upon a bough.
Leafy lives fill with the sap of all that's green
And *are* God's mind, whose code is in each gene,
And grow centuries of purpose into fruit
And show: soul ripens so new seeds can shoot.

We journey through a house and garden, shore

Up, improve, order and pass on the law   50
Of growth and fruit. The long way gives ample
If we soften to the universal
Sun. We journey, pick pears and paint old wood,
Teach sons. Seed is the end of parenthood:
The hard, small pear on the tree on the lawn,
And a ripe pip sprouting in a distant dawn.

Clouded-Ground Pond

On Strawberry Hill, a break in forest trees.
We park on mud and cross the road in breeze:
A brown pond, yellow lilies. It is cool.
We could stay all day here at the Horseman's Pool,
But it is near the road. We take the track
Past logs and stones in clay, turn into brack-
en, hawthorn, beech. And now, beyond holly,
A pond amid gorse and birch, and a fallen tree.

It has seen the agonies of the seasons:
How fathers died in autumn; the reasons   10
Young men married, were exiled, lived alone,
And their returns. This pond has also known
The stealings-up through sawing grasshoppers,
And secret comings far from eavesdroppers.
It has sensed small girls crouch in these gnarled roots,
And dreamt of the netting of speckled newts.

A touch of sadness taints the autumn tint.
Like a daughter leaving till spring, a hint
Of absence skips round the deep gravel pit.
Across its quiet eternal stillness flit   20
The changing shadows of dragonfly time,
Newt and lily months. Sticklebacks stir slime.
This gravel is honey, this cloud is cherry

And the heather and gorse smell of strawberry.

Now time disturbs the eternal with raindrops,
Voices. Ducks clack, dogs splash, a robin hops,
Frogs watch and plop in mud, a rustle rolls
Through the silver birch near where, in spring, tadpoles
Cluster like thorns round submerged sticks. At noon
The shimmering mirror, teeming with June, 30
Can blaze into nothing, while two hearts bound
As a face drowns in clouds to gasp on: ground.

Four worlds make contact in beauty, and when
The ground reflects a leafy, clouded sky, then
All four dance in the mirror of a pond.
Through layered leaves, the groundless soul beyond
Reflects clouds of spirit, and, in high moments,
The sun's divine air, blinding experience
Of the first source when all say yes and see
The One that shines within layered complexity. 40

Sadness and joy are one to this still *Tao*
Whose horn of plenty, like a watery bough,
Gushes buds, leaves, petals, and pours faces
From warm clouds into each self and all places.
Six months are one ripple that smooths away
All sad twigs till the dancing, wintry day
Restores a universe like a green shower:
The *Tao*-self renews the earth, stroking the hour.

As old genes teem new lives, *Tao*'s hidden sun,
Which joined the heights and depths and fused into one 50
The clouded ground, is now this lily, it
Gushes from clouds, is blown with pure sunlit
Wind, and rooted in mud, yet still, pours All.
The lily on-in water is a call
For Essex men to leave their cars and say "Yes"

To grounded roots in cloud-bordered stillness.

Two Variations on One Theme
1. Time and Eternity
(Second Version)

I held her hand at this Omega gate,
She wanted to paint the yew,
And now the moment has blown away
Like dandelion fluff on blue.

Now, on the High Beach forest church
The passing clouds and years
Are like pattering footsteps in the porch
Or the silence under bedsit tears.

In the city I am scattered like poplar fluff
Blown on the wind of echo,
But here I breathe, with the quiet of stone,
The white light these dead men know.

Oh bury me behind this grave,
At the low black rail,
That all who have suffered and been brave
May pass the yew and wail
For all whom golden hair enslaves,
Till the past is a squirrel's tail;
Then, like the boom in childhood caves,
Oh hear beneath the breeze
The mystery that flows through stars and seas,
Where the autumn bracken waves.

A Stonemason's Flower-Bowl

Near the Saxon church, a gate in the wall
Leads through pine trees to where shrill voices call.
Gothic turrets and arrow-slit windows,
Balconies for a Princess's rainbows.
Go in through the porch to a dark hall where
Old masters peer on walls. Up the long stair
Children swarm to dormitories in a tower.
Put down a daughter's case where shy girls cower.

This school was the Lord of the Manor's home,
And now, in holidays, town children roam   10
The lawn and woods that, from slit windows, roll
To the distant sea. Here descend and stroll
In what seems a permanent place. The town
Is new – our vandal century has pulled down –
But here four stone heads on a stone flower-bowl
Face four winds, like sad ladies round a soul.

For four summers she has holidayed here
And I have turned one woman to stone each year.
This town has seen the changes: crashing waves,
Four heads like capped bathers', four relief-graves   20
Round a flower-bowl life. In love a gorgon,
The artist petrifies all he looks on:
Here stands, like a breakwater Time foams round,
A monument, an artist's chiselling-ground.

This Sompting Hall, too, half hints at something
Half out of Time: it has a church bell's ring.
Towers and Tudor chimneys, structured, float
By changing seas, a changeless anecdote.
All castles and works of art on pages
Join all centuries, are read by all ages.   30
All stonemasons find things that never change,

And measure God by a distant mountain range.

The divine cloud that surrounds our stone ball
Yearns to ravish the empty minds of all
Masons who reach for mountains through grey skies
As if the Infinite were granite, sighs
For mind-travellers to: fly through their night-air
Up four worlds through rainbows; peer and soar where
A chink shines through the shell of our space-time;
Look through the air hole to the eternal prime;   40

Like astronauts squeeze through the airlock; float
Among timeless Ideas in God's mind; note
Bright images that flash down as events;
And bring four goddess heads back to blind sense
Which they, as careful craftsmen, curl and fix
In changeless winds and waves of stone that mix
Order and random hours on stone flower-bowls,
Give courage to endure to Time-bound souls.

Eternal images last, stones which show
Them seem durable. Halls sometimes echo   50
Turrets which an imaging soul has seen.
All else is flux: towns, women who have been
Made stone trophies round flowered beauty, seas, pain.
Bodies, like flowers, bloom, fade and come again,
Pass like returning bulbs in old urned souls –
Which are as enduring as stone flower-bowls.

Who cannot, then, lie on this sloping lawn
And open his imagination; yawn
And dream a summer dream, flat on his back,
Of goddesses, a sky like a mountain track;   60
And fix stones in the flower-bowl of his search,
Then rise and walk to the towering church,
Smell fading roses and, unflinching, stride

Where waves smash sea-defences at high tide!

Beauty and Angelhood
(And their Origin in the Fourth World)
(A Quartet)

1. High Leigh

Drive down the long drive to the ivied tower
Where the grand House stands, walk its maze-like lawn
With low wall, fields and trees, and warbling birds.
Here in the last war, Unesco was born.
But now it knows the bareness in the heart
For it reveals, like an old mystery school,
The "esoteric Christ" of hidden fire.
Will we find what we're shown, in a new Rule?

He holds the lectern, smooths dishevelled hair,
A Canon with charisma and fired sight: 10
"Don't teach the dead old forms, the skeleton –
Dogma or doctrine – but flesh and blood, Light
Augustine, John of the Cross, Teresa knew,
Christ." "Body without backbone," some growl, "wrong,"
But a rock-hard heart serves a corpse. Now thrill to hear
What we have known and waited for so long:

"The blowing from the spirit makes new forms
And shapes hard hearts in Christ-tide every day.
All mystics meditate on rocky mounts,
You should tread *your country*'s Mystic Causeway.   20
Let Indians be Hindu, your spark's Christian.
Churches should *be* the sea-washed Mount they preach."
Now walk the maze with him, catch fire and blaze,
Hear his urgent 'Follow me': "Come and teach."

He founded a sea-lapped Order that lives
The mystic stillness, peace and Light, quiet zest,
Has two retreats and hears tomorrow's call.
And all who went out East to bring the West
A contemplative rose which Europe needs,
From fire his Mass calls down, such men must know   30
New heat stirs in Church veins to renew soul,
As women wail to harps so souls can grow.

Here Beauty can be found, down these green lanes.
By this gate where sheep graze, be a skin-bowl.
As Lovers close eyes to open, here pause.
Get to know Beauty like a hidden soul.
Will there be entry to Beauty tonight?
Not while the thunder growls, winds howl and blow
Till rain hisses and explodes from puddles,
Not while light speaks from the sky to say No.   40

Morning. Eucharist, or "thank you". A priest
Fumbles at candles, which he cannot light,
Slops wine, shuffles, prepares squares of brown bread,
Prays words without feeling. Now rise and fight
To kneel at the rail, take "Spirit-bearing food",
Feed your spirit with the bread of life, be host.
He who calls fire to Mass has gone, but think:
This rosé is like blood for a tombed ghost.

Now in the library let the body
Be a Grail-bowl for Light through the priest's Lord's Prayer.   50
All cup hands, quiet, rise as the white fire glows,
Breathe down to throat this Light, breathe out dark air.
Thy will be done – let it come down to the heart,
Let it shape the heart into a Golden Rose.
Say "Come in God, come in" as flesh tingles,
Scalp prickles, hair stands up and tired skin glows.

White power surges through legs and burns darkness,
Volts probe each limb. Breathe in Light, breathe out love.
Draw Light as "daily bread" into the stomach,
Draw cleansing Light down into the groin, above   60
The red-hot rod which trespasses, cup hands
To the heart, draw power up to lips from earthed spine.
From the forehead raise it up, offer it back,
This circulating Light that makes skin shine.

Here Beauty can be found like a bare heart.
Sneak to her secret place from a hermit's room,
Lie down and love her lowered eyes, white fire,
Be a veined rock in the tides of her womb.
As Mount's Bay fishermen raise a crab-pot
From Tristan's Lyonnesse where coral blows   70
And thrill as drowned spires toll out hermits' prayers,
Beauty, I found you like a desert rose.

Desert. In a desert of council flats,
In a bare room sits a veined Rose in prayer
Whose Catholic hermit's power shakes Cambridge spires,
Whose beads turn judges pale, whose eye is air.
Evening. Leaving High Leigh is a going-down
Back to the world, but we have shaped the start.
The high places are gone, but we have known
Where hermits find the bareness in the heart.   80

2. Hawkwood

Sunshine in the Cotswolds. Drive up hedgerows
To the grey façade of a country hall,
Fields, iron railings, cows, horses, daisies.
Unpack above the old monastic wall
Where black monks still surprise old gardeners,
Then stroll among tall trees and quietly pass

Other silent walkers, listen for hawks,
Like a Romantic feed on leaves and grass.

The Kabbalah's sky-rooted chestnut shows
Beauty, the sun-like nut of all, descends   10
From germ down trunk and branch to bud-like Forms,
Manifests in the lake where downflow ends,
Blossoms into all beautiful things. Light,
Seen from hermit's eye, ramifies and teems
Unconscious images among green leaves
Which mystics tell, like candles, from day-dreams.

Now sit near a reflected Tree of Life.
The goat-bearded Teacher in sweater finds
Linked branches of triads and *sefirot*,
Grows *neshamah*, then *ruah* in our minds.   20
"Feel power flow round our enclosing circle."
Churn it on round like wheels of water-mills.
Though we are solid, we are like water
When our psyches convert to power that stills.

"Mirror images from the leafy world."
On watery mosaic, peacock and lyre
With hopscotch maze ascend a Tree of Life
To a large head of Christ and Crown of fire,
A Roman Jesus on a bathhouse floor
Near the sea, under olive trees. An ark   30
Hangs in a dark cloud while flames burn all round:
Merkava chariot in fiery dark.

"See Angels." They approach with veil-like flames,
Blowing like net curtains, visions that tease,
White brightness nothings where faces should be,
Five heavenly hosts fluttering in a breeze.
Then a large ring of celestial beings
With a dark centre, flame-like folds of veils,

And that black-hooded monk, no face at all –
Can Lucifer stay masked in such wild gales?   40

Lunch, then across green Cotswolds to Prinknash
Where an Abbot's house in a Tudor style,
Young Henry on wall, lodged on their return
The Benedictine monks of Caldey Isle.
Here is the Canon's quiet, but the Abbey,
Car park and tourist shop – such ugly 'charm'!
Is Christendom so enfeebled, the line
From Augustine to Eliot a bird farm?

Then back to "Inner teacher as high priest".
I hear my Angel say, "You have your task,   50
Get on and do it, restore the Mystic
Tradition within Christendom. Don't ask
Me any more. Bless you my son." And now
I know why I was shown the Prinknash mint
Where worldly monks have sought and lost Beauty
Too near coach park and shop – and need a hint.

When Goatbeard says "See this", images rise
In magic water, caught by magic art –
"As if a trawler's radar found a shoal
And filled its nets before anglers can start."   60
But poets hook visions from a deep dream,
How shallow is this small lake's *fishy* haul!
Did I see Angels or mere images,
Day-dreams or fantasies, not *ruah*'s trawl?

Though Tree helps understanding, I renounce
All reflections in waters as rungs up
To Tree-crown heights of all who saw Beauty
Not once but many times in a spiked nut-cup.
I will not have this magic round my will
For I have heard the Roche-rock mystic say   70

"Not 'my will' but 'thy will' is the iron
Ladder to the eyrie of the Mystic Way."

Now, raised from *neshamah* to *ruah*, sit.
As down four levels of a waterfall
See bright Fire foam and flicker and then lick
To rose, now golden flower, now a veil, all
Patterned, now turn to nut-heights of spirit.
An Angel in a cloud looks down, hawk's face.
High in this Tree-rock hermit's cell, above
Michael's chapel, know it is you and grace!   80

3. Kent House

The Canon in retreat. Walk past green fields,
Go past a wooded pond to a tree board,
Then turn off up to where the old ruin
Of an Edwardian House has been restored.
A tree grew through this floor and this ceiling.
But now, in this long room of easy chairs,
Sits a Community, and on the throne
Its Ionan Master of silent prayers.

"You can go on courses," he says, "and grow
Psychic 'shoots' in head – third eyes, clairvoyance –   10
Yet be choked in the heart, whose opened eye
Knows fiery Light of Spirit in one glance,
Airs pistil-ripe thought free from closed ideas
And the weed-maze of books that stifles brains.
Be still. Only the pure in heart see God.
Sun-warmed heart contemplates, closed head explains."

He talks like Zen Masters of head and heart,
Berates ideas and thought-patterns, scorns books,
Then puts us all in silence for a day

So we know how the hermit's spirit looks.   20
He reads Sufi tales instead of *koans*,
And urges us to weed the flower-bed.
Windesheim, Port Royal, Little Gidding –
I eat a lunch as silent as the dead.

The woods have bushes that obscure clear sight,
Thickets that snare the pilgrim from the corn,
Hide the deeper life from the noisy Way:
This murky pond whose still reflects each thorn.
As pond in woods is heart found within head.
Sink down to where 'I am' beneath all mind,   30
The still place of the spirit from past lives
Beneath all words and wants of loud mankind.

Great mystics mined their hearts like Cornish tin –
Engine-house, stack, then long Dark Night of Sense
Emptying rock of earthly images,
Shaft sunk to a deep level of silence
Where lamp-lit spirit finds veined Truth like ore –
Yet were still one with fiery divine air.
Now West's heart is like ruined East Wheal Rose:
A deep shaft filled with water and despair.   40

Beneath the slime of this foul pond, 'I am'
More than my body, emotions or thought,
And, poised in stillness like a water-gnat,
Beyond cloud of delusion this life brought,
Mirror a past meaning in detachment,
And wonder if this muck can be pumped dry
So the West lets go everything 'out there'
And lets warm sun shine on shaft mud, not sky.

In Michael's chapel, mystic life in deed!
"Deep in your freest recesses, see Light."   50
As sunlight probes the depths of Forest pools

A watery Beauty breaks our caddice sight.
Blind as Master brings spirit bread and blood,
Swallow and gulp, Beauty above heart's eye,
Ezekiel's fire. We revere flight in all,
But are these young grubs really dragonfly?

Mystic hatching to Light takes twenty years
And unpaid lads, "poor monks", are mere larvae.
"The New Age mystic life, unlike the Old,
Has evolved, comes unsought," is his reply,   60
"Has welled up in lay people, not *élites*
Whose books distract – I can tear up my book.
We do not need blueprints from past mystics:
Let spirit pour, don't feel 'Still years to look'."

He floods out past effort like a Red Guard.
Dogma, doctrine, now differences are drowned.
But I pump out, re-work, re-form, restore
The West's deep-mined tradition, and have found
Spirits, like mines, are not equally aired,
Doubt if his new wells have a Western role.   70
Can New Age dogma or can Kent House learn
From their Angel and cleanse the Western soul?

Can bread and wine and Beauty transform all?
Will this House's yearning reform the Church
So all altars, like candles, burn one Light?
Will lay folk sink church shafts for hermits' search?
Can this man with St Benedict's vision
Mine Europe to meaning? Lost in thickets,
Our dark Age crouches like a frightened child.
Look west to flooded shafts where Beauty sets!   80

4. St Peter's Convent

The country showdown. Turn at the gate, go
Through pines to the secluded convent where,
In front of Gothic porch and tower with cross,
A dozen old men sit and take the air.
This is a convalescent home now, run
By twenty-six old nuns and divine grace.
St Peter stands outside the chapel door
And looks in vain for girls to take their place.

Nuns excavate souls like a Mithraeum,
Then flame to Beauty, which sparks each Angel,   10
Spirits dug out like caves whose lamps hold fire.
Join dark flames for their Office at the bell.
As veiled, wrinkled hermits genuflect, see
Bare legs and buckle clogs from a lost age.
Spirits made flames who see One Fire, they are
Like the flame in sanctuary's blue lamp-cage

Or candles in Smeaton's wave-pounded tower
Whose granite tree turned cross with two-flamed beam.
Saturday *Feria* includes three psalms.
Singing quiet prayers for all near death, they seem   20
Dark Angels for the dying and blue light.
They file past us, their hands inside black sleeves.
We eat lunch in an enclosed garden, meet
The lady in whose scheme Peter believes,

Our agenda: a spiral for Kent House
(Correspondence courses, training weekends),
A "dance of consciousness" that may Paul-Jones
Beauty through Burrswood so her heartburn ends
A wallflower. Does God want *this* "new form" linked
To churches, does the Canon who repeats   30
"I want Communities throughout England,"

59

Appeals to lay masses, and scorns *élites*?

My dream is of a movement *in the Church*,
Of masses shown the Mystic Flame *in pews*,
Not "New Age" communes outside "old" churches,
A Steiner cult, dying out of the news.
The West is in crisis, the young cry out
For churches to beam out a wave-swept Light,
But, lost in dark, are rocked on Eastern sects.
What other Luther, Wesley, is in sight?   40

The meeting has begun, I must speak out.
The Eastern menace lowers like a storm cloud
And darkens all Christendom, which unites.
Let Europe blaze against the night, be proud!
The West longs for great mystics' quartz to strike
Steel-ruled spirits to sparks, so, kindling, all
See the world as One Fire, Beauty's blue Flame.
Christendom yearns, oh will you fail her call?

The Light has moved my tongue, I am at peace.
But who can see that far, the Dark Age pour?   50
The Light has moved me, but they cannot see
Revolutions destroy, reforms restore.
Remysticised Christendom? He replies,
"We must go on from here, not think of goals,
Take our pace and direction from the ground.
We are not ready for great mystics' souls."

And now I stand under the tower outside.
A dream has turned as sour as old men's love.
They wait in their wheelchairs to be taken
By veiled Angels back to their wards above.   60
Sour, sour as I watch Angels terrify.
Lovers, Teachers, Masters and Angels care
For body, mind, spirit or divine spark.

Angels care for all four while breathing air.

Angels have veiled heart, soul, spirit and flame
In this life or past lives, from earthly damp.
Angelhood is earned like a peerage for
Spirits flamed Grail-gold in Beauty's blue lamp.
God renews Church through Angels veiled outside.
Nuns see One Fire, give flames to souls in dark,   70
He serves new forms, I the old Mystic Way.
Old Church receives new life, old fire new spark.

Accept. Like nuns he shows 'cripples' the Light –
Invalids in wheelchairs – and does not ask
Why Michael spears the Dragon in Mount's Bay.
Farewell, silent Angel, I have my task.
I will build words like Smeaton's Tree-stepped tower
So all can know what lights a hermit's night.
Sadly I leave. A dream caught fire and blazed.
Now blown embers glow blue, Angels' blue light!   80

Crab-Fishing on a Boundless Deep

Go out in a boat in early morning mist
As fishermen put up sail, with a hose thaw bait,
Slice slabs of ray whose smear spreads through the fist,
Leave the Mount for six miles out, where gulls wait,
Where the bay is sheltered from the east-west tides,
Where crabs do not bury themselves in sandy spots –
In this autumn equinox each crustacean hides –
And winch up the first string of dripping crab-pots.

In the first pot, put down an arm and throw
Good crabs into a tea-chest; into the sea lots   10
With soft bellies, or crabs too small – no
Meat: dash and smash diseased shells with black spots,

Bait the trap with fresh ray, pile pots at the back,
When the string is done throw them in; with a knife, and Frank,
Nick each crab between each claw, and hear the crack!
Then drop it, powerless to nip, in the water-tank.

This sea which is so calm can blow up rough
If the wind comes from the south-east and whips
Water to waves, and this calm can be tough
In winter storms that keel and roll big ships: 20
The waves wash onto deck from the windward side
And fishermen need sea-legs to see-saw
High, stomach above the horizon, then slide
Down into a trough, as the boom becomes an oar.

This sea encompasses each horizon's tide
And we are alone on a dipping, lapping bowl.
This sea, which yields such crabs, on every side
Is an irreducible, inseparable whole,
Ebbing from east to west, pulled by the moon
Till it floods back from the west as the moon goes by.   30
Its tides make currents from which crabs hide in a dune,
This boundless water is ruled by a ball in the sky.

As so it is on land, that misty cloud.
Trees, earth, stones, rocks, clouds, water, air and fire
Are seen as different as each wave, as proud-
-ly separate, yet all are part of an ocean of mire
As indivisible as the inseparable sea
Whose waves rise, dip, and then return to the One.
I see currents of Existence pulled inexorably,
Till crops flood back again, by the moon and the ripening sun.   40

Both sea and land first came from air – from night.
As an unseen sun made Being's atmosphere
To unfold a world of currents pulled by Light
So our sun whirled a collapsed cloud to air –

The dust and gas which cooled into planets –
Whose cold froze molten rock, then melted seas
From ice whose water clouds raise as droplets
To fall as rain on hills, so that rivers please.

And now I see this vast expanse of sea
Is like the unconscious mind on which 'I' stand,   50
Which came from Being's air and sun – psyche.
And 'I' am this boat, my reason, ego and
Identity on a mind both vast and deep,
As wide as the world, as deep as the deepest seam
Of rock, pulled by a moon that is asleep
Which sets blind currents swirling through its dream.

Bait pots with the smear of time and let them slip
In this boundless, endless sea, then have a snack,
Then winch them up. Images claw and drip.
Take out the good ones, throw the soft ones back   60
And the small ones, smash diseased shells, then seize
Each one that will bite its own legs off with its claws
And nick it so it's lost its nip. Then sneeze
And toss it in a tank of crowded metaphors.

Then you can sell them to be devoured, this haul
Of Being's dripping symbols. Such small works
Epitomise the vast and boundless deep, so trawl
Where thirty fathoms down great beauty lurks,
Hiding in sand when the currents swirl and free
To emerge in slack-water between the tides,   70
And I'll pray that the Being that made this sea
Can yield its plenty up these dripping sides.

The Royal Masonic Hospital: The Nut within the Sun

Once masons built the universe in stone

And now the Tree fills their hospital's air.
Between Hiram of Tyre and of Abiff,
Who measured God with compasses and square,
Turn and look at the round glass mandala,
See Solomon on Jacob's ladder, and floors
With *"luf-knot"* pentagram, Solomon's seal,
And the dividers of Blake's God on doors.

Go up to the waiting-room, see the garden
And oblong lily-pond, papyrus plumes;   10
Where a fountain splashes time near a sundial
See the eternal sun peep where a lily blooms.
See balconies held up on stone pillars
As if four worlds were founded on the grass,
Go to the room where you will be nursed to health,
See sister's buckle, where set square and compass

Join pentagram in an eternal clasp,
The love-knot of crusading Templar knights;
Time embraces eternity above
A Babylonian-brick ziggurat's heights   20
Under which leaves flow up a chestnut tree,
Where images peep like brown conker nuts;
The architect of Solomon's Temple walls
Shows a Tree of Life rooted in the ark's struts.

As in King's College chapel, see through the stone,
Feel yourself in God's manifesting smile,
Restore the oneness between leaves and bone!
As wet papyrus waving by the Nile
Became the very first dry parchment scroll
So the chestnut Tree prints leaves in the gazing mind,   30
And brown nuts peep through spiked shells in the soul
And a sun bursts brown visions of one conquering kind.

At Penquite House, Near St Sampson's

I take the long hill path to Penquite House;
At the second gate, go down with barely a grouse
To a Victorian lodge, servants quarters and stores,
Past a gas lamp to the great double front doors
Where Garibaldi was received by Peard,
A Byronic soldier the Italians feared;
Round the conservatory to the croquet-hooped back lawn
And a view over where Golant and the river yawn.

Here the Barretts lived, and the Rashleighs too,
And other well-known families passed through.   10
Here is history among the thick hedgerows.
Now tired Youth Hostellers rest their legs, or doze,
Young men and trousered girls play pool or sit,
Bikes upside down, and dream of a love that's it.
I cannot ask to see Garibaldi's room
So I will imagine Tristan, stretched out in gloom.

I think of King Mark's palace at Castledore
Where adulterous Tristan wooed Iseult before
His wife's "Black sail" sounded like a divorce;
Now a ring of earthworks overgrown with gorse.   20
I look across the hills to the blue sea;
A superb place for a castle to be.
I stand by Tristan's sixth-century gravestone
With its raised "T", and hear Iseult's faint moan.

I walk down the path to St Sampson's church
Where Mark and Iseult made their devotions; I search:
No bats hang in the porch as they used to do,
I walk among arches and go straight to
The medieval stained-glass Sampson's cell,
His book, and the vision he had of an angel;   30
I gaze at the bossed ceiling the Colquites gave

And the vision that brought him to found this Cornish nave.

I go into the churchyard, look down again
On Fowey river and reflect on the two men –
Sampson and Peard, visionary and soldier, growth
As contemplative and man of action, both
Have a place in this magical countryside;
One settled by the well, one lived and died
In nearby Trenython, last years immersed
In the Bishop of Truro's panelling of Charles the First.   40

Sampson was of the time a fisherman saw
St Michael appear on a guarded mount, and pour
Visions to latter-day Sampsons, hermits
On Tintagel cliffs or in Roche rock's castle slits
Who lived on high in the Archangel's air
And hauled a basket of food up from somewhere
Below, and today who continues the visionary glow?
Not, of Peard's panelled house, the Bishop of Truro!

I think of Lanhydrock and Chirpy Richards' room
In the First World War, when he was a groom.   50
And the great life under the seventeenth-century ceiling;
I could be a visionary there, do my writing.
I will flee to my Penquite, make it a fort
And enjoy in its gardens away from the London Court
The contemplative life men of action crave, for
I too have been a soldier in a private war.

The spiritual and secular: Tristan, Sampson –
Both went to Brittany, one with a vision,
The other hopelessly in love, in pain;
Divine and human love, sacred and profane;   60
Like a soldier who fought in unifying wars
And an evangelist who Christianised with oars,
One needs the other. We conquer and love to make one,

And the mystic melts in God, the inner sun.

I have Peard, Tristan and Sampson within my soul;
Conquest, love and vision jostle, cajole –
The contraries within the heart and head;
Open to spirit and you channel it instead
Into the world of wars and love and sense
Where it pours in the workings of Providence.   70
We can live among opposites where we grasp, with a shock,
That spirit and sense are mixed in the Baroque.

Copped Hall ·

Turn off the Epping road well before dark.
A clearing leads to ornate gates, there park
And walk through pines past many a bluebell,
Over a hill till the great large-chimneyed shell
Of the third Copped Hall looms up, all overgrown.
Boarded up with corrugated iron and stone.
See the eighteenth-century pediments, as the light fades
Go to the tangled garden, and sunken balustrades.

The first Fitzauchers' hall passed to the Waltham abbots;
Then the King so Mary Tudor took Mass on this spot;   10
Then to Heneage (a present from his guest, the Queen),
Who rebuilt it and married the mother – hence the *Dream* scene –
Of Shakespeare's WH; to Suckling; Sackville;
Till Conyers built this shell that survived till
It was destroyed when a hair-clip used as fuse wire
As the household dressed for church, lit the final fire.

O Edwardian glory – four-columned pediment,
Italian gardens where walled terraces went,
Stairways, iron gates, fountains, figures of stone,
Parterres, summerhouses where caryatids moan,   20

Conservatory and ballroom, no clop of hoofs,
A grandeur of pavilions and domed roofs –
But now decay, a roofless shell again,
And desolation in moonlight, or this fine rain.

Alas for great halls, like this ancient seat
That stood against time and then crumbled to defeat,
Alas for past grandeurs like this stone shell
In which a style challenged the dark, then fell.
Salute the vision and energy of its prime
Which kept an estate going in a ruinous time.   30
As civilisation lost dignity, it saw
A way of life perish, now home for the jackdaw.

Now see the ruined foundations of Heneage's hall;
Elizabeth stood with Shakespeare by this wall,
And saw his *Dream* performed in the Long Gallery
At the wedding of his Theseus to Countess Mary.
How overgrown the yew walk now, climb through
To a ruined tower, headless marble statue.
Time, like a clump of nettles, winds about
Past glories and stings the hand that reaches out.   40

There are two forces – order and chaos.
Out of the forest: a fine house, gain from loss
Yew walks, stone steps, square gardens and statues,
And candles blaze against twilight's night blues
And a play is acted, all are in good cheer,
Then the ground moves and gigantic cracks appear,
The house is abandoned or razed, the people go –
Or else burnt down by fire, and the nettles grow.

But its scenes are retained for ever in these walls,
The voices that laughed linger as history falls,   50
Those images are present to our mind now,
We see a queen, a wedding, a frown, a bow,

And for all eternity each triumph matures
This Hall copped it from time, but its art endures.
Like Greek – or Roman stone, or art of Copt –
This ruin embodies events, as if time had stopped.

Oaklands: Oak Tree

I look out of my study window at
Green trees in chestnut flower, with candles that
Snuggle round a corner of green field, in the sun
On which blackbirds hop and two squirrels run,
Iron railings, where magpies and jays flit,
Where a woodpecker and a bullfinch sit.
Closer, two goldcrests swing near nuts, like thieves
And buttercups tint yellow between green leaves.

A Paradise, this field, where all aglow
I lay a childhood through a life ago,   10
Near the shady oak puffed at an acorn pipe,
And watched bees hum in clover when all was ripe.
A log, a pond, a horse, and everywhere,
Nature dances in the flower-filled air,
And among butterflies it is easy to see
A human gathers pollen like a bee.

A Paradise of sunlight and skipping feet
As swallows skim and swoop in the summer heat,
As a robin pecks in grass near children's speech,
The green only broken by the copper beech.   20
Here birds and flowers and insects perch and run,
And humans grow like berries in the ripening sun.
And tiny heads grow large like bud from stalk,
Like the spring bluebells fluttering round the Nature Walk.

It teaches that man is part of Nature's care,

That a boy can become a man without moving from here,
As a bud becomes the fruit of this apple tree,
Or this downy chick the nesting blue tit's glee,
As a grub hatches from pond slime into dragonfly;
This field is full of transformation's cry,   30
Of bees and birds and boys and girls and showers,
Observe your true nature among these flowers.

See the great oak like a druid tree – divine,
Filling with acorns that will make a *soma* wine,
And give the sight of the gods to all bound by sense,
Who see merely social faces across the fence;
Your true essential nature must include
This Tree of Life that pours spirit as food
Into the world, like acorns into leaves, and feeds
A horn of plenty that pours out souls like seeds.   40

At Hatfield House

I walk through the maze of gardens, and look at
The south face (Inigo Jones), and retrace my steps
Back to the Old Palace – old brick, wood stair,
And, sitting on a lawn among marble statues,
Suddenly as the birds sang, I caught a glimpse:
The studded wood door opened and a figure glided
Down the wooden staircase to walk in the miniature maze,
And out to the wild roses, and the twittering birds,
And I knelt and said "Your Majesty" as she passed.
O marvellous places that have such memories!
I can reach you Elizabeth, in the places where you walked.

Greenfield

Greenfield has mountains all round it,

And trees and hills where whitethroats flit
Beyond a bridge, where black-faced sheep
Baa in bracken, and brown cows sleep;
On its green slopes town men can graze
Till social eyes see with soul's gaze
And feel with trodden celandine
Or swoop with swifts, rejoice with pine
Where eagles fly, and midges swarm,
Or fish for trout (wince with hooked worm);   10
Town men can share country delights
During the days or the light nights,
And climb Ben Nevis when it's clear
Or drive and sample Highland beer
Near where the rose-bay willow-herb
Pinks every wayside's floral kerb,
Visit castles if days are full
Or disappear to Skye or Mull,
Or see glass blown, or flower-press,
Or look for monsters in Loch Ness,   20
Or draw water from Garry Loch
When burns have dried to bouldered rock;
In Laddie Wood, under Ben See
Deer dart across a path, then flee.
Near mountains wrapped in mist or clouds
Far from all noisy coach-tour crowds –
Green days in sun, red faces glow,
Log fires that blaze when night chills blow;
Bees hum in harebells, and men fill
Quiet, tranquil hours in a deep still.   30

Iona: Silence

By ferry cross blue sea to green cliffs where
The grey Abbey stands out. Once ruined, it
Is now restored. Dolls' houses, we grate on the pier.

I walk from white sands to where whitethroats flit,
Look back at the deep blue of each Northern wave,
Then glide on grass through the roofless nunnery
And a pilgrim now, feel where nuns who gave
Up mainland charms went to their church in glee.

The path winds on to St Oran's chapel. There
I sit in twelfth-century quiet – two pews   10
Under a light, and a carved hearth – then peer
At kings' tombs in the Street of the Dead, and choose
St Columba's shrine, which two wheel-head crosses face.
I sit where his tomb once was in a still like sleep
And feel the energies of this ancient place
And sink into silence on which baa sheep.

Here I am at home, apart from the outside day
And noisy children – or a singing choir;
Here I can sink into deep quiet and pray
Where Christendom began in Columban fire,   20
Go back to the roots in silence of our free
West. Here in Nature's beauty I feel the hour
A culture put down roots like a growing tree
That feeds our leafy consciousness with still-living power.

I find the grassy site of Columba's cell,
A doorkeeper's small door in Paradise.
By the Abbey altar where Columba fell
I sit, feet chilled on ancient stones to ice,
And feel the earth's power surge up through each limb.
I stand again before St Columba's shrine;   30
The cross that has a druid's sun as a rim
Throws its shadow through the door in the sunshine.

The shadow of the ringed cross is on my back,
Feet on the earth, there's a tingle up my spine,
I lift my target-ringed heart so I soar till – crack!

Light breaks, prickling my scalp, flooding my shadow line.
The Light is in me, I am in a trance inside,
I surge and feel the heart's love burst in heat,
Full of the Light's orgasmic power, I glide
On a silence that has seen heathen hordes retreat.   40

Where else in Britain can one know in shrines
Religion is contemplation, not hymns in a church,
The truth Zen masters know in mountain pines?
I know Columba, who killed in his saintly search
Three thousand men (sense and spirit indeed!),
Who sailed thin coracles in a whipping breeze
And stamped a hermit's gaze on the pagan creed
And loved the beauty of these Northern seas.

At Tintagel: St Juliot and Merlin

I leave the Land Rover and walk down the scree,
Then climb the cliff path past green turfed rock, run
To the low slate grey walls that overhang the sea
That is clear green in the midday August sun.
Groined caves lurk below me in the veined headland;
I climb up steep steps carved in rock, windswept,
To twelfth-century castle ruins that stand
Where King Uther ruled and Queen Igerne slept.

The grass is steeped in Arthur, of whom no trace:
The Norman castle, Black Prince's great hall,   10
And further up a tunnel, a food place
Carved by some Celts in the solid rock wall,
And further on – breathtaking views – a well,
Eighteen feet deep here near the cliff-top broom
And, with fifth-century walls, a Norman chapel
And an altar that was a Celtic tomb.

⌐And here I start, among the grasshoppers and,
Skipping in lilac heather, the tortoiseshell,
Looking across at the keep on the mainland
For here St Juliot came from Wales and had his cell,   20
Before St Columbus or Benedict.
I descend to the site of the Celtic monastery where
I sit in a low-walled hermit's cell (strict
Rule), the sea spread beneath me, green and clear.

Here I am at the very beginning
At the time of the Desert Fathers who sent hermits
Through Gaul into Britain. This simple living
Precedes Arthur and the reason for our visits.
Here there was barely room for a man to lie
Down, but he was above the world, near God, at one,   30
Open to the winds and the ocean in the sky;
In his inner dark he could see the midnight sun.

I sit on the beach below by Merlin's cave,
Where Uther's son was handed to the old wizard
Or druid. I sit in a crowd who misbehave,
Not controlling their dogs, shouting each word,
And in this babble of twentieth-century noise
These shrieks and cries as if Uther had died,
I think of Merlin's solitude and poise
(His cave's escape to the bay the other side).   40

I think of the hermit perched on his great height.
O wonderful place that has Juliot above Merlin!
Dark caves of magic, and hermit cells of Light!
Wizard king-maker, and hermit denying skin!
Magicians are in the world though apart from it
And use their powers to scheme within the Whole.
Hermits are above the world in the Infinite
And purify the world with their praying soul.

At West Ham: Saved by an Artist

You came round with complimentary tickets, so
You sat in our sofa and chatted, and I put
It to you, "What if there's a penalty tomorrow?"
And you said, "If he takes it with his right foot,
I'll go to my right," and at the match you slouch
Till just under the stand where we sit, your guests,
A Watford player is tripped, and so you crouch
As a blond international runs in; as if beating their breasts,
The hands banging the back wall stop in fright
And all is silence as you dive to your right.   10

A roar! And we're on our feet shouting "Yes",
Forty thousand hands stretch to the air, we shriek
For you have the ball, a brilliant save, no guess.
Tears well into my eyes, I cannot speak,
Washed through with the emotion of the crowd, whose roar
Thunders and reverberates around the stand.
The relieved ground cascades applause and awe,
But you seem apart as your captain shakes your hand.
Your save kept Watford out, and so all sing.
West Ham have gone to the top and so bells ring.   20

And now I know, as I reflect, I will bear
That moment and emotion to the grave –
The ball from the boot suspended in mid-air
As you begin your fall to your right to save –
A moment frozen for eternity,
One I shall remember in thirty years' time
As now, ball hanging from a cross, I see
A diving header, a goal and a cup-winner's climb.
Memory mixed with emotion is image,
And remembering revives the emotion like a bridge.   30

And my boys will remember your save when they are old

As I recall Denis Compton's tousled head
As he danced down the wicket before the ball was bowled,
Sitting with my father whose domed head is now dead.
Some moments – a four I hit or saw, a wicket,
A nodded goal I watched or scored, your save –
Assume a bright pattern in the carpet
Of all I did with my life, which I take to my grave.
You made a memorable save and I feel as purged
As by catharsis, when pity and terror have surged.   40

And now, on Sunday, you bring autographs
And I know you know that life is about more,
As you sit and chat and drink my wine, with laughs,
Than kicking a ball goalwards and trying to score –
Is it really so important for crowds to chant?
Are the prancing preeners mad? Are the players stars
When they earn a wage from a game of chance, and grant
That all their skill can quickly end in scars?
You live for applause in fading afternoons.
What are you without a leather ball and goons?   50

We sit and talk, you know we are two souls.
You want to be a coach or insurance chief.
Panis et circenses. You give men goals,
Like a therapist, you tense and give relief
And let the crowd's roar fill their head and hand
And excite their blood, cleanse them with their own, "Yes"
As the eternal purges the things of time and
Leaves them flushed with surges of emptiness.
You are an artist, you create an image in time,
Sculpt a deed like a sandcastle in mime.   60

Now you have gone. You have left your wife,
Are living "in the car", have taken your clothes,
A credit card, a front door key, a life.
You have taken out a mortgage that she loathes.

You were a fallible god. I cannot believe
You are a violent brawler under the moon,
That police have been called to your home. I grieve,
And choose to remember your deed that afternoon
As twenty thousand held their breath, then leapt
And applauded an artist, hands over head, and wept.　　　70

Rainbow Land

As I drive home towards a thundercloud –
Behold! A bright rainbow arched in its pride,
Rising out of Greenwich, reaching to the heights,
Yellow in the middle, indigo, red outside.

I marvel: it has come out of nothing;
Sun on icy rain. So it is with bright
Vision : sun on bits of experience.
From Tower Bridge Greenwich is bathed in visionary light.

It is so bright, and a trace of another bow,
Apollo's, now shafts through a church clock's hand
It recedes as you draw near. May I long remain
A fugitive like this in rainbow land.

Worthing

A green sea smiles by breakwaters
And brown seaweed, a hazy sun
From which I squint. Tiers of wavelets
Breeze on shingle, wash in and run.

A gull drifts. Windbreaks and flags flap,
The sound of the sea is like the wind
In leafy trees, non-stop, it gusts

And waps this canvas, shakes what's pinned.

I, Sisyphus, pause from rolling
My boulder up the barbarians' hill,
See a smiling face in the universe
And am at one with the infinite will.

Rough Stones like Monks

I cross the ancient stone causeway,
Laid five hundred years ago
By French monks after Edward gave
This Mount to a Mont that could glow.

Up through drizzle to the low cloud,
To the castle crag again
Where long ago St Michael appeared
In light to shocked fishermen.

In a cloud like a mist, an ancient church
Stands on the North Terrace and
I am in a cloud of unknowing
Where I cannot see land.

But can see around the battlements
And here within this cloud
See the rough stones cemented like
Monks bonded in a crowd.

With Harold at Waltham

I walk through the stone arch, and by the stream
Which brims over the weir, plunges into gloom,
And beside the Abbey to the old altar's dream,

Now in fresh air, and stare at Harold's tomb.
Here Harold was brought, identified by his belle,
Edith Swan Neck, after the arrow in his eye,
Here he lay by the nave he built, as the old order fell
To the Norman horde – French Danes with a Latin cry.

The last of the Saxons. Under Canute the Dane
A carpenter had a dream that all should dig   10
Forty cubits for a buried cross, it sounds insane
But a black flint crucifix was found – quite big –
And the Lord of Waltham, Tovi the Proud, inflamed,
Claimed it as treasure, loaded it on an ox-cart.
The oxen only moved when Waltham was proclaimed –
Then people were cured, blood gushed from a stone like a heart.

Miracle or superstition? Accident? Providence?
Tovi vowed he would serve the cross and fate,
And his lands passed to Athelstan, his son, and thence
To Edward the Confessor, who gave his estate   20
To Harold Godwinson, on condition there should arise
A monastery there – we stand on holy moss.
Harold was broad, tall, handsome, strong and wise,
And cured of paralysis by the holy cross.

The finest man in England was elected King
And beat the Norwegians at Stamford Bridge, but then
Prayed here before Hastings: the figure, bowing,
Looked down from the cross sadly, an ill-omen,
The Saxons rushed on William crying, "Holy cross."
The cross disappeared in the Dissolution, and yet   30
In this oldest Norman church, I still sense loss,
I can still sense Harold and the Norman threat.

The cross – a dream, superstition, miracle, shield?
What can we make of it now when so many doubt?
Carpenter guided to a hill, a cross that healed,

And the Doom painting in which Christ sits and looks out
While two angels blow trumpets and the dead rise
From graves and are weighed in scales near a demon choir –
Was this the old order's folly? Look with Bayeux eyes –
The Normans were superior in their Roman Fire. 40

Greensted Church: Martyr

Drive through Essex hedgerows filled with desire –
Cow parsley with red campion for a bride –
To a wooden Saxon church with a wooden spire.
Upright halved tree-trunks from the nave outside,
A porch with roses, but inside recoil:
A stained-glass window of St Andrew bound
On an X-shaped cross; look back, in quatrefoil
The head of St Edmund, on a martyr's ground.

The stained-glass window shows his fate: the King
Of East Anglia when the Danes arrived, so fierce 10
He refused to relent his faith in Christ, praying,
Was bound to a tree and shot – with arrows that pierce-
-d his side, then his head was cut off with a sword-heave
And thrown into bushes, where it was found
Being guarded by a wolf who would not leave
Until it was rejoined so he was sound.

Much later his corpse was moved, and rested here.
See the beam has a crowned and bearded head
And a dog-like wolf. And so this church, which seems bare,
Made from trees like the Tree of Life and fed 20
With a Saxon eye-hole niche and leper squint,
Celebrates the tree to which St Edmund was tied,
And despite its water stoup it gives a hint
Of the criss-cross trunks on which St Andrew died.

The Saxons worshipped pagan gods "in groves"
Until St Cedd converted them to Christ,
And the West huddled and grew round Dark-Age stoves
Until the Danes came with Beowulf's *zeitgeist*.
O hail the red-cross martyrs who endured strife
So Bernard, Teresa and John of the Cross could illume.   30
What courage to place a faith above one's life
Like the Crusader bowman under his shield-shaped tomb.

Martyrs put a cause above themselves, they live
Not hoping to see the outcome of what they do.
Martyrs affirm the faith for others, they give
In an act of love, a choice between false and true.
As Christ hung on his cross, Edmund on his tree
Rose above his executioners and their might;
His severed head, like Orpheus's sings free
A call to all to follow what is right.   40

I walk, stunned, through tents with aromas' lures.
It is the herb festival, a hundred jars
Proclaim "nettles", "marjoram" and their cures
To people who believe herbs cure like stars.
How many here will stand against our Danes
When they come with their arrows, helmets and shields
And load our bodies with barbs and a conqueror's chains?
May we have Edmund's courage in our green fields!

At Dark-Age Jorvik: The Light of Civilisation

We drive through a flat green Yorkshire countryside
And sit in a hotel room, overlook the Ouse
Between two bridges and the pale Minster,
To which we walk along the Shambles, choose
The medieval butchers' street, and think
Of the stink and how many fires have spread,

And look at Clifford's Tower where the Jews were killed
And see where Richard of York was beheaded
And where his head was stuck on Micklegate.
York is a town steeped in history's hate.   10

It is the Vikings we have come to see:
Jorvik, lost capital of the Danish myriads.
I think of the first raids and the settlements,
The attacks on monasteries by sea-nomads,
The capture of York by fiery Norsemen
Who beat Anglo-Saxons who wore helmets
Like Oshere's of Coppergate, the raiders who
Imposed Danelaw and levied a thousand debts.
My name is Old Norse, and my family, though dead,
Had Scandinavian looks, and a long head.   20

A personal journey, I sit in a time car
And travel backwards in time to the yells
Of a Viking settlement of timber houses,
A farmyard everyday life, child cries and smells.
The wood stall cups and bowls, the bone carver,
The jeweller's and leather shops and leather shoes,
The coopers, the woman with plaits among geese.
Now into a house, where round the hearth they use
Two men sit and talk and cook and weave,
Bend by the fire under hanging bags, and believe.   30

Suddenly an echo reverberates:
I too, once sat in a half-lit gloom like this,
Amid cooking smells and a woven wattle wall,
This crowded filth, these clothes – something I miss.
A race memory or a hint for a former life?
I sit by a fire, hear gibbering in Old Norse,
Stop playing chess-like *hnefatafl* and tense,
Know war is near, a conqueror without a horse
Yet an outsider – we keep ourselves apart,

As I do now, from the Anglo-Saxon heart.   40

The glimpse has gone, but I know these Viking men,
These sea-nomads, addicted to food, girls, ale,
These earthy bearded men who mend nets, cut
Oak planks Norman fire will char, sew a sail.
I know their manure fork, bone antler combs,
Their spindle whorls, toggles, pins near their chests,
Their iron coin dies, men's pointed leather caps,
The short-sleeved underdresses low down on breasts –
I have like Beowulf drunk, before a log fire,
Mead ale and gazed at a fair-haired wench with desire.   50

And I know the religion of these Viking men,
Their cult of Odin, the god of death, the shield
In battle (German Wodan, Anglo-Saxon Woden),
Who welcomed dead heroes from the battlefield,
And of Thor the thunder god, and his hammer,
And their runic inscriptions on wood and stone,
The spells and curses in runes Odin gave men,
I know the shamans who gave them their own
World Tree on which Odin hung, pierced with a spear,
That road to the Other World embraced without fear.   60

And I know the Christianisation that happened
As the Vikings tried to win the Church's support,
Not challenging the Northumbrian religion
Which proclaimed "The Lord God is King", and fought.
We had St Peter coupled with Thor's hammer.
While Odin, pierced with a spear, hung on a crossed tree.
I saw no conflict between the two, we were mild
As the Christian vision retained its supremacy,
Imposed on the invaders' cult with outstretched arms,
Encouraged by us invaders' Viking charms.   70

Now I sit in their triumph, the Minster,

Which shows the glory Christendom has been;
The pillars soar to arches and gold bosses
See the stained glass, the Kings on the stone screen.
The crumbling and decay cannot conceal
The growth that thrust this glory to its height,
Why did we not Vikingise Christendom
So Odin and Thor triumphed over Christ and his Light?
We raiders lacked numbers, no King came round
To Odin, who lacked magnetic strength on the ground.   80

Civilisation triumphed – another way
Of saying the ambience transmitted growth;
From Charlemagne, a thrust carried us forward
And spurred Crusaders to keep it in their oath.
I think of my coat of arms, the Crusader's cross
Grew Europe better than the hammer of Thor,
The Light of civilisation beside which
The Dark Ages seem times of night and war.
Soon the cross which inspired this Minster turned
The Vikings into barbarian raiders who burned.   90

So what were the Vikings we all can recall?
Dark-Age savages who scratched at the soil,
Marauders who pillaged and raped and lived by power,
Northern Huns who left nothing behind their toil.
They had no social church or creed or belief
Which attracted martyrs or seers with bent backs,
And so Odin on the Tree became Christ on the Cross
And Thor with his hammer Saint Olaf with his axe –
Fit to be Christianised by the Light in the soul
That brought rose-windows in stone and a Gothic control.   100

Question Mark over the West

After Fernhurst we turn up a wooded lane

And drive across Lord Cowdray's estate till
A three-gabled stable cottage and urbane
Line of chestnut trees, facing a wooded hill,
With honeysuckle over the front door.
I stand near a French drain with my cousin and gaze
Across sheep wire and mounded mole-hills for
Wild life, and potter in the house and praise
The white-wooded windows and life of a squire,
Then sit in one wing at the birch-log fire.   10

And now at night a deep peace in the dark.
We stroll under a brilliance of stars and swoon –
W of Cassiopeia, Plough like a question mark
Or sickle in the sky – and gaze at the moon,
A cusp on its back above a line of firs
And I smell the sweet smell of the earth, digest
The moisture of woods, this idyllic quiet that spurs,
Wonder at the question mark hanging over the West
Like a sickle set to recapture lost ground
And scythe all Western gains without a sound.   20

The rabbits have eaten the growing shoots,
A fox escaped the hunt up the hill somewhere,
An owl sits on the fence-posts and hoots,
The baaing of new lambs fills the evening air;
A green-topped pheasant sits in the green field,
I hear a gun's report, a squirrel runs
A hare lopes among hedgehogs; may the gun yield
To the bird by the chestnut fencing. The Englishman's
Country life is as old as Chaucer's day,
The sweet smell of the earth has its own way.   30

Who would think here of a threat to democracy?
This remote lane through a lord's estate, these woods
Keep at bay the bad news on the TV,
The darkness round our sickle moon, our "coulds".

We who threw up computers and man's quest
Through NASA saucers and voyaged through a comet's trail,
We masters of chips and reason master our West
By carrying homes on our backs as we work, like a snail.
I see the Plough fall in a shiver of stars
And a question mark scythe the fir-trees to stubbed bars.   40

Before the fire and flintlock guns, we recall
Our roots in our grandmother's garden,
The shed we scooted to, where Percy stood
Over the grinding wheel, sharpening knives,
A fir and frogs in a cellar, the sunlit grass,
"Shut this gate" wood with primroses to each knee,
A bomb blast at the gate and shattering glass;
We made the best of forties austerity
Like the arcade minstrel doll with a hand held out
Who popped a coin in his mouth, we never went without.   50

This Sunday country air at six hundred feet,
Is heady like wine; we walk past suckling lambs
Up the wooded hill to Northpark Copse and greet
A crack down the blue sky to where a feller jams
Felled chestnut trunks as fencing poles in the ground.
I look between the Downs over the Weald
Towards Black Down and the Pilgrims' Way, which wound
From Winchester to Canterbury across field,
And then we plunge down to Verdley Edge and the chime-
-less clock in the woods that measures a timeless time.   60

The air is scented with spruce and pine tree,
We cross the road, climb to Henley through beech
Where a stream splashes and pours down the hill, and see
Ears of bud, crocus and snowdrops gush and reach,
Sip draught cider at the Duke of Cumberland
By wisteria, wheel and post-horn, gaze and doze
And watch dark trout dart, turn and dash, get canned

By the pool that collects the spring and overflows
To trickle and splash and gush down the road
With a freedom that our land has always showed.   70

Over cheese and chutney sandwiches we talk
Of how you settled here – but not how, looking at Mars
That first spring day after a five-mile walk
I saw the night fall in a shower of stars;
Of the peace of a family inside their fence,
Each individual free in the scented air
To think and talk and be, without interference –
And to open their hearts to the One in each easy chair,
So that pinpricks of light pierce from on high
Into this one ball, the mind and inner eye.   80

Lunch is finished. At four a wet mist sweeps
Up the valley, the horse edges towards the poles
On the leaping flames in the farm as the dark creeps.
In this peaceful country life men find their souls
And live in the shadow of the moon-like One
And go to town to work the West's machines
And then return to enjoy the quiet, the sun,
Or go to the ancient Norman church, grow beans,
Graze sheep under the crooked crozier of the Plough,
The shepherd's crook that hangs in the night sky now.   90

Cotswolds: Winter Four-Sidedness

Moreton in the Gloucestershire Cotswolds, a skin
Of Regency windows, and peace like a spire.
Here Jane Austen might have walked, here in this inn
Charles the First slept a night, by the bar log-fire
Which leaps invitingly through the freezing glass.
In the back courtyard a fountain squirts and falls,
Icicles hang baggy round its trickling pass

Like the cold brittle poems round my spring's walls.

Broadway in Worcestershire, a quaint wind-blown
Village of old houses, removed from power,   10
In a long lined street of yellow Cotswold stone
And behind it on the Beacon a great church tower
Where a fire was lit to warn of a dangerous threat
And where Byrne-Jones walked with Morris in a gale.
We visit a vicar in double-glazed quiet
Then go to Evesham across the snowy Vale.

Chedworth Villa, a first-century Roman's dream:
He saw sheltering hills and a sweet spring for
A thermal bath with 'central-heating' steam
Through stone toadstools that held a mosaic floor.   20
I look at the mosaic Winter with his hood
(*Birrus*) and tunic, holding a branch and hare.
Perhaps this Roman Briton owned the wood
Before the Saxons drove him out somewhere.

Burford. Near the Wildlife Park, a scare:
A blue car in front swerves across the road,
I see it hit the verge, spin through the air
Three times, bump a stone wall upside down. Slowed
A red car swerves round it and drives at me.
I brake, it swerves back. I stop and get out.   30
An elderly man, blood trickling from head. He
Lifts two stones from his lap, stained. Eyes doubt.

After this intrusion, the Cotswold peace has gone,
The quiet, the antiquity of stone and moss.
Bourton-on-the-Water, three low bridges on
The Windrush. Stow-on-the-Wold with stocks and cross,
A church where Cromwell locked up a thousand
Royalists – I keep seeing that car spin through
The air, blood trickle down that head and hand

As he staggered from his car as if to queue.   40

Now I stand by the four-shire stone, twilit,
In winter east of Moreton, and I think
Of the four counties I cross as I walk round it
And of the Western spirit, and I link
To a Winter four-sidedness, and see
Fine art, domestic peace free from ferment
And civil disturbance, scenic beauty,
And Providential protection from accident.

Ode: Counter-Renaissance

I hurtle down the M3 like a lord
To the Saxon capital, Winchester, and pass
Alfred who holds out his guarding sword,
Then, early, linger by Cathedral grass,
See the site of the Saxon minster's aisles,
Then go inside to look at St Swithun's tomb,
Canopy and catafalque, and ancient stones:
Saxon knights, Norman arches, medieval tiles,
Reformation bishops, Caroline hair, Victorian room –
This history begins with Cynegils' holy bones.   10

This tradition wrested a hope from death,
Like Bishop Fox's corpse, which he carved to stand
For mortality and urge humble breath.
St Cuthbert holds King Oswald's severed hand,
In the mixed-up bones in chests of the once crowned
Which include Canute. Ribbed figures lie, fresh
Mouths gape on tombs in images of hope.
These ribbed, recumbent men in marble found
The invisible body within decaying flesh,
The letter within the outer envelope.   20

The tradition is there, which fifteen centuries kept
And there is a practice with it, on the hour
As a black-frocked priest ropes off the north transept
And singing voices waft into the tower;
A practice that, like mould on a forest log,
Feeds on antiquity, but yet smells stale
To all but the connoisseur and naturalist.
O living history, damp in evening fog!
I hear the Hallelujahs, and like a snail
Creep off to await the lifting of the mist.   30

And now I arrive at the nearby college where
For nine years mystics and scientists have met.
And a spiritual presence is in the air
And confronts materialists with an uncertain threat:
Bits of magic clutter the reception hall;
Crystals, charms, trinkets of a superstitious time.
I leaf through books on soul, wince at the weird,
And stare at people who strut and pose and sprawl,
Who wave their hands and know we have to climb
And smile under berets, all posture and white beard.   40

Some stand at the lectern, one by one, and shine;
A white-haired man calls for a new Renaissance.
There is little imagery for their line
Save the diagrams on the wall and their own stance.
They cite the lore from books, and boldly shout
"This cannot be proved by 'the intellect',
You must imagine the spiritual is here,
The reason is bad, do not take notes." They spout.
(An hour of Pan – if only he could select!)
All have progressed from editor to seer!   50

With mounting excitement white-hair scythes the air:
"Science lifted us from medieval theorisings,
But ego, with the sense-bound body's flair,

Cut us off from spirit. We are spiritual beings
Housed in the temple of the pure body,
Sparks of divine fire, remember who you are.
Don't believe this, but live with it today,
Imagine you have an immortal eye
In your divinely designed body, say 'Hurrah!'
You are not an accident of chance or play.   60

"A deep psychological change affects each art;
When the arts renew contact with the divine
There will be a new Renaissance of the heart,
That will outshine the fifteenth-century sunshine.
We are on its threshold now, for we are open
To a flooding in of power, light, thought, romance;
We are being transformed from sense-bound wit
To divine beings lifted, as by oxygen,
To the pre-Fall mind – a Counter-Renaissance
That takes us back from body to spirit!"   70

It's a new movement within the tradition, a late
Going-back on three hundred years of Darkness,
I walk in blossom and meditate
With this white-haired giant who shines his "Yes",
And leave behind my body and fly through a hole
To a Garden of Angels, a pre-Fall place,
And float in my invisible glowing form;
"All Nature is unfulfilled till the human soul
Unites with its being," he says from inner space
As the Light beams in and leaves me feeling warm.   80

I kill Darwin with Sheldrake and then shrug,
And now his wife talks on the vibrating world:
Her Mongolian chant can smash a jug
For sound decomposes matter when it is curled,
I sit and make my body into an ear,
And vibrate like the ringing of a gong.

91

Forgotten-about knowledge pours in from the air:
"The higher mind when we attune and peer
Is like fish turning in shoals," or like a throng
Of migrating swallows wheeling above Leicester Square.   90

Now Sheldrake talks to me of goals in my room,
Teleology Darwin did not know;
Of purpose in creature, atom, star, and womb,
How the Western lack of tension must go,
How spiritual intensity thrives in war
Conditions, not comfortable surfeit and scorn,
Not in the liberal West that lacks an aim.
I say the new Renaissance will restore
To a world that is Western wherever suits are worn
A rekindling of mystic goals – the Flame!   100

I walk among trees at blossom time and feel
The rutting sweat and shudder of passionate love,
Know ambition to make money. This zeal
For the sense-bound should not be sneered at from above.
Celebrate the opposite of decaying flesh –
Bodily health! These grey-faced ghosts that stroll,
These spirits before their time, are sheltered from shock.
As man discovers his spiritual being afresh
Let him also love and earn – and be healthily whole!
Sense *and* spirit – world *and* beyond: the Baroque!   110

I return to the Cathedral and its Saxon kings,
The holy relics that healed, and in the crypt
The healing waters that cured the skin's red rings –
Was not sense known in each clerestory manuscript?
I think of the West, which Hermeticists deride,
As being in a cheap reductionist age –
Woe to the civilisation that will not allow
Scientists to explore within as well as outside:
Bishop Fox carved his own skeleton's corpse, the sage,

To remind his soul he should be humble – now!   120

Two hundred billion stars in as many galaxies,
And does Providence guide despite this dust?
The Dark Age is round the corner, and it is
Human agency that will keep the West robust
And reunite its western and eastern shores,
Unify the world in a new image of man,
The spirit in sweating flesh that loves from afar
Like the winged Guardian Angels where this chapel soars –
O Saxon knights in stone, awake and scan
And fill with angelic light this tiny star!   130

At Cartmel Priory: Taming the Unicorn

I enter the Priory where black-habited monks,
Augustinians, kept a sub-Abbey with a smile,
A lamp under chancel arches like tree-trunks
And *triforium* stones whose Norman style
Arrived late in this backwater, this glade,
("Transitional Norman" it is called), until
The Dissolution of barbaric Henry made
The roof fall in, this art to be damaged, and shrill.

I wander the fourteen-fifty choir and gaze
At the Renaissance screen where pillars show   10
Emblems of war – crusading swords, the blaze
Of a tunic cross, gauntlet of ring mail – 'grow'
Among the crucifixion (hammer, spear, nails,
Ladder) and the true vine, the life and law,
And I think of my crusade through Christendom's gales
And am troubled by my own crusading war.

For I have struck a blow at the infidel –
And shattered a hostile tyrant's HQ

Where he co-ordinated fifty terror gangs well,
Have unmasked his secret design, his private view,   20
And now he is rampant, quite mad with scorn,
And I am like a stoner's pile of stones,
A lion fighting the dangerous unicorn,
A beast that retaliates and spikes one to bones.

I wander restlessly, and start in the gloom –
A reminder of my mortality, I stand
On a skull and two crossed bones on a flagstone tomb,
And an hourglass with moments like grains of sand
And wings which show that time is winging round
To the day when I too will become, undone,   30
A skull and two crossed bones under the ground,
Struck down by an assassin's murderous gun.

I reflect posthumously, a lingering ghost,
Was it worth it? To accept martyrdom?
Yes! For an anti-Western army, a host
Of two million would assault our land and bomb,
And there were few who recognised the war,
And few who would stand up and take the risk, the best;
I did not flinch to attack the murderous four
Who would destroy with bombs our sacred West.   40

I think of the attack that must surely come,
The smash of the bullet into the brain,
The leaking of blood on the flagstones, flesh numb,
As the unicorn turns savage, and spikes again,
And seeks to impale all with its white horn
And I await in a Priory church bloodstains
As Becket awaited his four knights who, sworn,
Sliced off the top of his skull and spilled his brains.

I wander back to the choir and gaze
At the misericords on the choirboy seats,   50

The grimacing devils and holy saints in a daze,
And suddenly by the opening my heart beats
For I see an oak tree and a unicorn;
The tale's hunter has dodged behind the tree,
At which the beast has charged and impaled his horn.
The oak tree has captured the unicorn, I see!

And now I am light-footed as I tread
On the two crossed bones, skull and winged hourglass
And gaze at the loaf on the tray, the bread
Put out for the poor each day while centuries pass,   60
And now I watch sheep crop the tumbling graves
And climb the Gatehouse, once near the convent part
And the prior's manorial court, and my mind behaves,
Now I am resolute and firm of heart.

We are on earth a fleeting time and act
To improve our age in a small or major way,
And we must not flinch from death, which is a fact.
We define ourselves against the dark, each day.
Then others carve our names on our tombstones,
And our deeds are recorded for others to read and see   70
And the crusading lion does not rejoice with moans
As it captures the unicorn in an oak tree!

Castles in the Air

Warwick Castle, turrets and battlements,
Finest medieval castle for earl and liege.
Take the winding path, admire its gaunt beauty.
Inside the portcullis think of each siege,
Walk through the private rooms, State apartments
Yet this fortress was Warwick's home, and task;
The Chapel built by Greville, State dining-room,
The Great Hall with its armour and Cromwell's mask,

Bonnie Prince Charlie's shield, paintings and statues
Where the Kingmaking Warwick made known his views.   10

Admire the cedar panelling, the tapestries,
Chippendale chair, a rare French clock cajoles,
Marble Florentine tables and gold ceilings,
Silks woven from Lyon, rose-water bowls,
Red and green drawing-rooms, the blue boudoir,
Van Dycks, Henry the Eighth after Holbein,
A fourteenth-century staircase lurking near
Opens for secret messages – the hot line:
A boat down the river, a horse across fields means
Affairs of State are solved behind the scenes.   20

All Europe is in this fine country house!
It is a work of beauty, intricate, detailed,
Perfectly proportioned, a pattern on life's flux,
History everywhere, the spirit is unveiled.
I could gaze for ever at Ann Boleyn
And her sister Mary, when Henry took a stroll.
This richness that edifies and exalts
Sends the heart soaring and uplifts the soul.
I wish I were an aristocrat, I who
Am a connoisseur of what spirit knows is true!   30

And now the lake side. I climb to the Watergate Tower
Which Fulke Greville's ghost haunts after his foul
Murder by his servant. Now the torture chamber,
With its rack and head clamp, foot screw and howl,
The dungeon with its chains and *oubliette* pit.
Poitiers prisoners sat in a dark still,
Wall stocks. On to the capstan guardroom where
Edward the Fourth was imprisoned by Richard Neville.
He had Henry the Sixth in the Tower – Kingmaker's bones,
How history cries out of these forbidding stones!   40

Beauty and cruelty are to be found here,
The beauty of a cruel, oppressive past.
I see Elizabeth visit Warwick
On the way to his brother Leycester (the favourite last).
His father Northumberland had lost his head,
After Jane Grey's queenship, in Mary's Hell.
How did he greet her four hundred retainers?
What a miracle the sons survived so well!
Elizabeth loved Dudley, the Queenmaker's son,
Whose stepson Essex rebelled and was undone.   50

I go to Kenilworth a few miles away,
A reddish ruin with bluebells on the walls
And a Norman keep, which Cromwell's barbarians sacked
For the Warwicks always answered Royal calls.
The towers open to the air – clouds pass across,
Old Gaunt's first floor Great Hall is a ruin now;
Superb square-topped windows, which Dudley built,
Hoping to be King, and the hearth is still there, somehow.
And here are the windows where Elizabeth stayed,
For nineteen golden days in heat and shade.   60

O royal lovers in our Golden Age,
Your spirits are here in this romantic glow.
The moat has dried, but I can see "R.D."
On Leycester's gatehouse, and his Tudor stables show
The esteem in which he held his fairy Queen.
Birdsong now fills the trees, as you hunt to the horn.
O how you tried to please your would-be bride –
You set up a Hospital for the poor on the lawn.
I pass it on the way back, it is still in use
And the Queen kept her head, and let you loose.   70

I leave the two brothers, go to Charlecote
By the Avon where a Tudor-style gate-
-house shows Sir Thomas Lucy, with spade beard,

Dog, falcon and family, the magistrate
Whom Shakespeare crossed as he killed deer (Shallow)
Two years after Lucy killed Edward Arden.
What fine paintings and furniture adorn
This Lucy's house: Tudor wine-cup and pen.
Kingmaking Shakespeare looked at this landscape:
The green field by the river, the field of yellow rape!　　　　80

The Heart of England has a wild beauty:
Castles intact, preserving all from fate,
And ruined palaces where ghosts now meet.
Why should this distant past still fascinate?
We are as we are now through our fine past,
Which shaped each art, set standards for all time
To which we now imperfectly aspire,
Which we hand on before our midnights chime.
Civilisation gilds rough *objéts d'art*
And makes magnificence where there were *faux pas*.　　　　90

And so accursed be the Cromwellians
Who tore down Leycester's love, for their own time;
And may we live among the past's splendours
As by the Avon, we chant Shakespeare's rhyme.
The soul is fed by beautiful artefacts,
Art nourishes the soul, is its psychic food,
So to live with the art of a great tradition
Will keep the soul vibrant and pure and good.
These battlements and ruins escape their hour
And feed my soul, for castles in air tower.　　　　100

Bluebell Wood

In a beechwood full of green
And last year's golden leaves,
In a sea of bluebells

A woman bends (white sleeves).

She is gathering logs
For a May fire (white hood),
Unaware of the blue
That glorifies the wood.

So it is now with me:
I toil and do not see
The silver birch nearby
And the tide of blue near this tree.

At Gunwalloe: The *Tao*

A blue sky, green turf on cliffs, a calm day,
But as I sit on this rocky promontory,
Hair tugging in the wind, feet splashed with spray,
I am the surging of the mighty sea.
Waves curl and hang and dip and explode and boil
And foam on this once molten rocky tower;
A haze hangs over the tranquil bay, I coil,
Am taut with frothing white and swirling power.
The winds, the sea, the earth have motions that
We take for granted till we wake in shock
And gaze at the headlong dash and boom-thud, at
The conflicting stillness of this glistening rock.
Two opposites are reconciled in spray
In the haze on the still blue sky of this surging Cornish day.

In Gough's Cavern, Cheddar

Enter the dark of a Cheddar cave,
The limestone has hollows like cheese,
And stalactites still wet grow from

A million years of dripping ease.

The deeper you go in, the more
They assume man-made shapes and sprawls;
There are: St Paul's Dome, Organ Pipes,
Solomon's Temple, Niagara Falls.

Now in the dark Druid Chamber,
A cat prowls near the light, coal black,   10
And now there is a Swiss Village,
Church and Castle on a mountain crack.

It reflects the ceiling above
In still water that runs gently
From the river Yeo which trickles from
An underground lake like the sea.

The heart's tongue fern grows when the lights
Are on, bringing warmth like the sun,
There are horseshoe tufts in the rocks
Which pulse with the energy of the One.   20

Here images sleep near a central sea.
Each cave reminds me of the heart,
And phallic stick-ups vie with what
Imagination suggests through art.

Each cave reminds me of the heart
And I think of the candles at Wells;
And oh for a flame like Jesus' love
That would light this cave, cleanse its foul smells.

It is now filled with horseshoe bats
And lurks with menacing shadows;   30
And when there is a light in the dark
It softens the dripping of time, which glows.

The flame of love burns in the heart,
Shines in the dark, without ceasing to be,
Burns brighter for being offered to others,
Throws shadows across the cave walls of "me".

By the Chalice Well, Glastonbury
(A Contemplation)

Avalon is like an earth goddess on her back,
Great breast and nipple, pregnant tum, raised knee;
Ponder how you disembarked by the lofty track
Up Wearyall Hill, as if from surrounding sea,
And saw by the windswept thorn, once Joseph's staff,
The misty isle of Avalon stretch and reach
Down to the Abbey fields and the Tor's top half
To this Chalice Hill and the Pomparles beach.
    That ziggurat drew Neolithic crowds,
    A tiered world mountain bulging into clouds!   10

Here height corresponds to depth, as mountain tracks
Reflect cave-paths down and up a rock-face.
At Wookey Hole descend to the Styx-like Axe
Which pours from deep within the caverned place,
Then go down from cave to stalagmite cave, for
Hell is a dark seven-ringed tower upside down
Which mirrors the seven-layered maze of the rising Tor
That corkscrews up and thrusts its sunlit crown.
    Height-depth, Light-dark are linked, like Heaven and Hell,
    As on the two-circled cover of this ancient well.   20

In your mind ascend the Tor and gaze from the top
Round the once-flat waters of the dried-up marsh.
See hills rise from St Michael's Tower and drop
With the last Abbot, and be quartered, a harsh
Fate. Admire the scales and St Bridget milking her cow,

Then descend to the house of Tudor Pole
Who saw Oneness and bought what is here now,
Visit his rooms, enter this garden of soul
    And sit by the waters of this chalybeate spring
    That runs from within the Tor and heals suffering.   30

Ascend four levels: the water-splashing bowl;
Up through two yews to the arched gate in the wall,
Past daisies and a red-berried shrub, stroll
To the splash and tinkle of a reddened waterfall
And iron-red runnel and Pilgrims' Bath; there dwell,
Then up past a yew to the Lion's Head; there drink,
Then pass two thorns till you reach this silent well.
Is the Grail that caught His blood buried here? Think,
    Does it stain these watery channels a healing red?
    Is there a Lourdes-like healing at this well-head?   40

Four worlds in garden levels approach this grid:
Here under two berried yews three steps of stone
Lead down to a chained, wrought iron and wooden lid
And two overlapping circles which can be known
As the seen and unseen worlds in a *yin-yang* whole,
Or male-female, conscious and unconscious mind.
Stoop and open the doorway to your soul,
Look through the bars, leaves float where old bricks wind.
    In Roman times the ground was near the base
    Of this well, and the spring ran through this holy place.   50

Here sit and recall the past, how He was here,
The boy Jesus who came by boat to mine
With His uncle Joseph of Arimathaea
And take back Priddy lead for a Roman shrine;
How he later returned and built the first church
And how He held the Last Supper in a room
At Joseph's house, how the cross ended His search,
How His uncle buried Him in his own tomb,

Then fled with the rest of His disciples, and the Grail,
And Mary, to live here beyond the Roman pale.   60

Travel in slow mind, linger in the crypt where
Joseph was buried under the Lady Chapel and
See the Abbey before it became ruined air
(Turf on arched windows), wander and stand
Outside under the Jesus Maria stone;
Think, Mary too lay in this floorless void,
And think of the others who became bits of bone
Before the wattle-and-daub church was destroyed;
    Near Joseph and Mary, know why it is said
    That Avalon means "the Island of the Dead".   70

Ponder the best-kept secret of the Christian Way,
How Joseph's altar tomb with quatrefoil
And shield, *caduceus* and stone JA
Was moved from the Abbey in Puritan turmoil
To the parish churchyard, thence inside the church door
Where now it is topped with glass and a funeral pall,
And stand before the relics of one who saw
The face of Christ. Did it grace the Templars' wall
    As the Turin Shroud (they claim) from the Garden Tomb,
    Which they copied onto wood in Templecombe?   80

All that was then, it is now we must renew,
So sit and be the moment in this evergreen!
Be the green oak fountain against the blue,
Be the hovering hoverfly and all that's seen.
Be the drifting ice of the tide-drawn cloud,
Be the rose that glows red to the reddening sun –
Be the translucent rose! that lurks in a shroud.
See how the whorls of your forefinger run,
    And gazing at the whorls round the grassy Tor
    Let the Light shine through your whorled and grassy awe.   90

⌐I close my eyes and am filled with a surge, now a lull.
The Light is in my limbs, and behind my face,
A sun-like circle interlocks my skull,
Haloing my shadow in this quiet place,
Here in the birdsong of this October evening
I am each bird, insect and flower. Here see
Eternity as an ever-flowing spring
And feel your soul as a well that can catch, and be,
    And store the spring-like powerful Light that rose
    Within the great Tor, in a high world where Void flows.   100

I see a man with a water pitcher pour,
I see the waters of spirit pour through the air,
I see all nations drink at this spring near the Tor;
No more the fish, the Aquarian flood is here.
No *Vesica Piscis* where two circles meet,
Where two worlds energise the spirit's thread;
The soul like a circular well traps Light's round heat
And pours its healing as from a Lion's Head
    That cures the body like Lourdes, fills soul with power
    So Eternity flows through a wall and through every hour.   110

The Romantic Revolution

Did Coleridge come to Wookey Hole,
And see the Axe pour out
From the underground Wookey caves and
Hear 'Kubla Khan' like a shout?

I go to Nether Stowey and stand
At the green front door aglow,
Where the person from Porlock stood,
And peer through the curtained window.

And I go to Watchet's old port

And see the lighthouse and hill,
And gaze at the Methodist "kirk",
Which the mariner knew when ill.

And now at Alfoxton House
I see where Wordsworth stayed
And pondered *The Prelude* on his couch,
Till a revolution was made.

And I feel close to both of them,
And can almost share in their walks;
I find them through their quaint houses,
And reconstruct their talks.

And they soon lose their mystery,
And lead me like a guide:
The mariner and the caves of ice,
The Prelude, the countryside.

Their great poetry revolution
Was a friendly affair
That grew out of visits to places,
And they then built domes of air!

Gog and Magog

Gog and Magog – just two
Ancient oaks that survive
Of an Avalon avenue
That led to the Tor like a drive.

The rest were chopped down in
Nineteen hundred and six, and
Many had seasoned rings
Numbering two thousand.

Gog and Magog's huge trunks
Show a girth unlikely to fall,
And are honoured by druids,
"Lovers of the oak", and by all

Nature lovers who feel
The oak is the English tree
Whose acorns once made cakes
For a mystic mass of the free.

Hedgehog in the Wild

I went alone to the field.
There by the oak-tree log
Weary and hungry lay
An exhausted hedgehog.

I took him to my house
And gave him milk and bread,
He sniffed, then sat in it,
Lapped round his prickly head.

I made him a nest of leaves,
I nursed his health with a glass
That held carrots, lettuce,
I tickled his snout with grass.

The next night I ran to his box
To give him his bedtime milk –
But o, my hedgehog had gone,
Climbed down my table nest's silk.

He is out there in the cold
Roaming the darkened hill,
Looking for those he lost

When I seized him against his will.

St Olaf's Church

Under snow-capped Scafell,
England's highest peak, sun-kissed,
Is England's deepest lake
Wastwater, eerie in mist.

And here within yew trees
Is England's smallest church,
Elizabethan diamond windows,
Pews for thirty-nine to perch.

It is St Olaf's church
Three Viking beams across,
Which came from the wreck of a ship,
A dreadful Viking loss.

At the inn see Will Ritson
England's biggest liar peep.
I measure truth by the snow-
-capped height and sparkling deep.

Full Moon on the Pennines

On the bleak moor the wind is keen
And bites below the ribs.
An old slate pub with a two-door grate
Warms for the dales, or fibs.

At Barnard castle above Teeside
And a splashing rill explore
A window near the round tower with

Richard the Third's four-barred boar.

At Bowes' west end stands Dotheboys Hall,
Low-windowed, edged by moon,
Where Nickleby suffered under one
Less generous than I with a spoon.

And at High Force brown water slides
And cascades seventy foot down
And foams on boulders through ancient trees
Whose roots cling above one's crown.

And I am back at the divine source.
As a full moon has uncurled,
I disturb rabbits and pheasants
Above the moonlit world.

The Yorkshire dales slide up and down
The mountains rise to cloud,
And I have left contemporary life
To know God in a shroud

Who can warm hearts like two-door grates
Open the mind like a tune,
Rush down its cleft like a waterfall
And shine like a Pennine moon.

A Viking Inheritance

On this Trelleborg heath, this starting-place for wars,
See the round green banks with four openings
And the markings of square houses in fours
Which housed Svein's twelve hundred much-armed Vikings.
Two rivers wind for the sea, where the long ships wait,
And we embark for England, to harry towns

For silver to pay the fleet. Piled stones by the gate,
Now sheep graze thistles, clover on these downs.

Wander in this Heorot-like hall of toasts,
An upside-down boat, crossed timbers at each end,   10
With oak-carved tiles and thirty outer posts,
See the tables before the hearth, the feast and friend-
-ship as men drink mead, hear heroic deeds and yell
Until they fall back asleep, their spears and shields
In the end vestibules that keep out dread Grendel.
House martins flit from the roof, swoop low on fields.

Now at Roskilde see the Viking fleet
In its glory! A deep-sea trader soars;
The curved prows of a merchant ship, so neat;
A wide warship, see the holes for the oars;   20
But just look at the length of this long ship,
It could take a hundred men and was used to raid
And even now fills me with terror. I see it dip
As it heads for the open sea and the English "trade".

It is a heroic time, chieftains buried
In graves marked out by boat-shaped stones, or in
A ship as at Ladby, the Viking pyramid.
The Aggers of Aggersborg, to a deafening din,
Glide off for England to pillage towns, to look,
Settle with English women, to be confirmed   30
As lords of the manor in the Domesday Book,
Living on the Danelaw fringe, as it was termed.

From the Cobb, Lyme Regis, 1988
(Or: 400 Years On)

A cloudless sky, a summer's day,
The sea is calm and washes in;

Ancient homes bask in the sun and grin,
The cliffs are green across the bay.

And from the Cobb jutting out to sea
Five men o'war drift out to fight,
The galleons of the Armada's might
Which puff their red-cross sails to lee.

A harbour-master's cap on crown,
A boy directs their course beneath
Where on Grannie's 'carious teeth
Jane Austen's heroine fell down:

Forget that there on Monmouth beach
Twelve rebels danced on a gallows,
Their heads stuck on church spikes by foes –
Memories that wash in and reach.

All Lyme is full of joy this day,
The waves sparkle, dazzle the soul,
All creatures flash out from the whole
And smile to exist by this bay.

The Dead Poet Bids Farewell to his Mourners

Now a life is ended,
Hear the wisdom of death:
A thousand moments fade
Like a cloud of frosty breath.

O all you who are gathered
In this old Forest church,
Look out of the diamond windows
Where the beech and silver birch

Reach for the whirling clouds,
Wave in the dying sun,
Rooted round the graveyard
Where all the dead are One.

Know that I'm among them
And camp under reaching leaf,
I rise and float at night
In a mist that knows no grief.

My heart is in the Forest,
I roam alone and free,
A cloud of consciousness in
Sunshine of eternity.

Being's Shout

The chestnut fountains its white,
Its candles glow and preen;
It was bare just two months ago,
Now all is teeming and green

And waves in the remote breeze
Which blows from the Milky Way
And with the sun and the rain
Makes everything grow each day.

I am a chestnut tree,
My candles of words shine out,
I wave in a divine breeze,
And exist in Being's shout.

Elemental Sea

The wind is whistling and roaring tonight,
Flinging fountains of foam a hundred foot high,
Washing along the harbour wall, waterfalling down,
Lashing the window, blowing in clouds of spray.

A hurricane is blowing in from the sea
And I am elemental once again,
I sit among the winds and booming tides
And cower from the storm like a caveman.

This cavernous home on the edge of land
Is buffeted by winds and mountainous seas
And I delight in the frothy turbulence
That rages round the peace of its timeless days.

It is good to receive a hundred smiling guests
And then drive down to this timeless hermit's cell,
Perched on a cliff, and watch with a seaman's eyes
Till the whirling clouds reveal bright stars: the All.

Good wine, laughter and the merriment of friends
In a hall with a Christmas tree make one forget
The fountaining of an elemental sea
And a hermit's glimpse of what Is and is not.

Stillness and Tides

Hundred foot waves round Porthleven's Clock Tower
Have smashed the quay. How fared the church on the beach?
I drive down the narrow lane, where the sea's power
Has left pools of water within the grey sky's reach.
The bay is white with surf and boiling foam
Which splashes on black rocks and a clean shore.

I take the sandy path as to a porched home.
Sandbags; within, wet tiles, wet wooden floor.
O wind that blew the sea at this church's inside,
O invisible power behind the winds that surge –
How could you destroy what a saint has toiled to raise?
Or does the invisible force behind wind and tide
Wash into old forms this new age to urge
Men to renew the symbols of their still gaze.

A Man of Winds and Tides

A Cornish sea captain with a grizzled beard,
And weather lines round his elemental gaze.
From the cliff he gazes at where the horizon's cleared
And slowly says, "There be rain later, and haze."
He knows the weathers and can steer by stars:
"Orion's three-starred belt, there: his top knee's Rigel.
His bottom shoulder's Betelgeuse – not Mars.
See the triangle down to bright Sirius – he's well –
And up to Procyon. See Regulus, and Pollux too.
Up to Aldebaran, Algol and Capella.
To the Pleiades, and Cassiopeia's 'W',
And the Plough's two pointers to Polaris, the Pole Star."
He lives among winds and tides and does not know
Quick town-men envy his being, which is slow.

Snow, Peace

All night it snowed – all's white,
The grass, the roofs, all clean;
And the world that was dull is bright
With an iced cake's frosty sheen.

Icicles hang from the eaves

As I blow on my hands and write.
Railings, fences and plant leaves
Support eight inches of white.

No bird moves, all is still
And my whitened heart is at peace.
As more snow flecks the chill
I am one with when I will cease.

At Polruan Blockhouse: Soul and Body

Like a guard in this ruined blockhouse,
Looking out across the Renaissance bay,
Winching up a chain to stop all boats
And collect their tribute, and their pay –

Like a guard in these ruined stones,
Wandering from window to hearth,
Which he shares with the keen west wind
And the honeysuckle up the path,

I, my soul, in this ruined flesh
Like this butterfly, this herring gull,
Beating in these ruined bones and walls
Flutter in my imprisoning skull.

O flying soul, you are happiest
Out near this calm wide, sparkling sea
And long to escape this prison and know
The oneness known by a bumble-bee.

Tall-Masted Ships and Woodpeckers

Two tall-masted ships in the harbour,

A two-masted brig on the sand,
Its hull being painted this low tide;
And a square rigger in the dock. And

Two green woodpeckers sit on the lawn
Of this pink house; green backs and tails,
Red striped heads and speckled bellies,
As rare as rigging and old furled sails.

Tall-masted ships and woodpeckers –
Both things that are now rarely seen;
They bring back a century ago
When trees meant decks and roads were green.

O mechanisation! Today,
Iron cargo boats and holds in foam
Preserve the woodland trees and rides
Where woodpeckers can nest and roam.

Smeaton's Tower and Western Civilisation

"Except the Lord Build the House They Labour in Vain That Build it"
(*Psalm CXXVII*, Inscription in Smeaton's Tower)

From Plymouth Hoe a tranquil sea,
In the blue sky a dazzling sun,
Like Drake I finish my game of bowls
Before I make the Armada run.

Drake waited for the tide to turn,
His piracy had provoked Spain,
His coolness hid self-assertion
And an Empire built on the pirates' main.

Now I climb Smeaton's eighteenth-century Tower,

Ninety-three spiral steps to a glass box   10
Where twenty-four candles shone to ships
In Victorian times from the Eddystone Rocks.

Each stone was measured exactly
And rowed fourteen miles out to the light
And winched into place with pulleys
So it fitted exactly in breadth and height.

And when it was later replaced
The light was dismantled stone by stone
And re-assembled, in a perfect fit,
Here on Plymouth Hoe to be wind-blown.   20

Hail engineer Smeaton's precision –
Now a wartime Spitfire loops its loop,
Diving down over Drake's Island,
Dipping its wing to the Tower in a swoop.

In our civilisation great events
Are not forgotten, are like a shrine.
They shine like the light on a lighthouse,
A cool response, an exact design.

A civilisation is a spiral
With a staircase like Smeaton's Tower,   30
Its base is in a Golden Age,
A Light shining through its sea power.

On Smeaton's Tower an inscription reads
"Except the Lord Build the House They
Labour in Vain that Build it." Our
Light-based civilisation was built this way.

Our civilisation once carried a Light
But now, like Smeaton's empty Tower,

Its glass chamber stands empty
And the Lord who built does not light the hour.   40

Will no-one relight the lamp that lit
Our civilisation in its Victorian time?
We need to restore its tallow candles
And learn the lesson of Smeaton's spiral climb.

Mermaid of Zennor

Enter St Senara's old church
In Zennor's rural street,
See the nude medieval mermaid
Carved on the side of a wooden seat.

Long tresses cover her bare arms,
She has no breasts that I can see,
She kneels with a pure fish's scales
And fins where her nether parts should be.

Half woman, half fish, she is Christ
Who was half man and half divine
(Or Christian fish). Her two natures
Recall his two natures that shine.

She holds a quince, or love apple
Like Aphrodite, and a comb for her tress-
-es. The quince has become a mirror
Of vanity and heartlessness.

This mixture of love and nude scorn,
Of Aphrodite and Jesus
Are both in this kneeling mermaid
Who is human-divine like us.

Copper Beech: Fountain and Fire

The copper beech still fountains down
This early November morning.
Leaves yellow-orange, like droplets,
Cascade and tumble with much foaming.

The copper beech curls like a fire
Licking, flickering as it dies down,
Blazing downwards in a glory
Consuming in gold orange-brown.

The copper beech will soon not pour,
Its copper flames will soon be out
But within my soul it will foam on,
A fire that knows no fall or doubt.

Reflection and Reality

From this dark harbour wall
In a rock pool nearby
A round cold yellow ball –
Horus' reflected eye.

And high in the night sky
Above the copying beach
Ra's round cold yellow moon –
The real beyond all speech.

The rock pool is now dark
A cloud covers the moon,
The real and its reflection
Are one in a dark dune.

Time and the Timeless

South London: tower blocks,
Fly-overs, traffic lights,
A mesh of railway lines,
Chimneys and building-sites.

The Surrey countryside:
Timber frame, Tudor bays,
Cottage, farmhouse and barn
Along Merrie England's ways.

I live in a tension
Between this new and old.
Everywhere I observe
A conflict that leaves me cold.

The concrete that renews
Is judged by ten thousand rays,
And o the juxtaposition
As a civilisation decays.

Tin-mine near Land's End

A tin-mine on rock cliffs,
Dusk at Land's End.
A chimney like a tombstone
Where bones descend.

A shaft where tin was mined
Ores from the earth,
Gleaming in shiny rock
Where ideas have birth.

I mine my unconscious for

Images of tin,
Until, as in a tomb,
I am buried therein.

Transient Existence and Lasting Being
(Or: Lasting Things and Transient Things)

"Time is the order of the succession of events"

A pier with Victorian lamps,
A man with a bending rod,
A shivering mackerel,
A mist that is moist with God.

Mountains and misty woods
Of lasting Anglesey,
And the pointed Byzantine domes
Of this pier speak to me

Like the rare butterfly settled
By my feet with outstretched wings,
And the tide that flows and swirls,
Like the wind, with transient things.

Transient things shiver
Like wings and tails, then die;
Permanent things of stone
Reflect Being on high.

O Victorian lamps and domes,
Ephemeral butterflies,
O pier and fish-filled currents,
What lasts is where time flies.

Leaves like Memories

The wind is high today,
Whirls leaves like snow;
The gold copper beech leaves
Fountain and glow.

Autumn is in the air
And in my soul.
I shed gold memories
And become whole.

I am a tree, am bare
Structure and bough;
My leaves past memories
I recall now.

Split Ash

I drive across ploughed fields,
Through gold and russet trees,
To the sweep of Parndon Wood
Where the dead float in the breeze.

Your name is in the book.
I walk to the split ash where
Eleven years ago
You forked away into air.

Three rooks glide like dead souls,
A squirrel scampers by.
I wonder in the stillness
Where we go when we die.

In this sacred oak grove

I have turned from noise and talk
And sense your dead presence
Behind me as I walk.

A chimney, a split ash
And life is split from death.
Here angels glide and soothe
And still each griever's breath.

Flow and Flood

The wind is blowing tonight;
I lie in bed and hear
The gales buffet this house,
Roar in the chimney and tear.

The neap sea pounds tonight;
In bed I count waves fall,
Thunder onto the beach
And boom up the sea-wall.

O lift the curtain, look;
White crests fountain up rock,
Break over the harbour wall
And spray lashes the dock.

Surf boils near the Hotel steps,
A lone boat dips and bobs,
A gull hovers hindwards,
All Nature dances and throbs.

This tearing energy
Quickens my breath and blood.
All Nature is in a flow,
I swell with passion's flood.

The wind and sea tear in;
My love, feel this thudding heat.
Let us lie in bed and count
Each breath and each heart-beat.

Think, body's and Nature's tides
Obey one vital flow
Until the flood is spent
In one last panting blow.

Harbour-master

When Graham was Harbour-master
He knew every inch of the port,
The boats came in within
An inch of what he thought.

When Graham was Harbour-master
Even a rough sea learned.
It boomed up the sea-wall
So far and no more, then turned.

Now he is gone, I look
At the raging sea's progress
And fear it may flood this harbour
And reclaim us like Lyonnesse.

Rain Globes

Rain globes on the rose-bush,
Globes hang along the wire;
Birdsong this damp morning,
A January choir.

Crocuses nudge through grass,
The spring is in the air.
Green woodpecker and moorhen
Move in the field and stare.

New life is coming through,
Pushing up through the earth,
Pushing through winter dead,
Pushing into floral birth.

Rain globes on the rose-bush,
Each like a world, they spin
And twinkle in the sunlight
As a blue tit glides in.

Long-Tailed Field Mouse

As I cleared our front porch
And the *débris* of years and boys,
I found a nest in a shoe
And opened a suitcase of toys –

Out jumped a mouse and ran
And hid under steps – "see him?" –
Then ran and jumped on a wall
And sat, bright-eyed and slim.

A long-tailed field mouse –
I identified him, and then
He was up the bank into shrubs
And gone under leaves again.

O field mouse I am sorry
I disturbed your cosy lair.
You were welcome – the universe

Is for all beings to share.

Poet and Snail

A snail outside my house –
A slug with two thin horns
And a round house on its back
And the freedom of hundreds of lawns.

You travel with your house
As you trail, like a free man –
Like a gypsy wanderer
Who writes in his caravan.

Sea-Shanty

In the dock the *Maria Asumpta*'s
Rear sail is raised, and a man sings
A sea-shanty above the quiet waves.
From the deck his lone voice warbles and rings.

In my room, polishing my poem, I stop
And listen. His voice drifts out to sea.
I too am singing to the wind
In the hope that someone will hear me.

Midnight Sky: Hawthorn and Almond

From the pier the midnight sky
Is an umbrella of great height
That blew into hawthorn spikes
And now leaks points of light,

Or like an almond tree
With blossom, that has white
Petals down all its boughs
And shines against the night.

Invisible Tree

Above the roundhouse mast
Some stars dance like fireflies
On a great fir-branch that is hung
With fairy lights, in disguise.

The biggest, brightest stars
Are like globes on a lead
On an invisible tree
That supports a structured deed.

Peering Face

The bottom half of the moon,
Round half up to a bar,
Orange on the night's horizon,
Huge and seen from afar.

As I drive, a great oak tree
Passes across its space
Like a silhouette on a lantern
Held by a peering face.

At Otley: Timber-Framed Tradition

Flailed hedges bud, corn shoots are a lush green;
The Suffolk countryside has burst with spring.

As I drive up Hall Lane the brown woods screen
The four tall double chimneys and nuzzling
Gables of this studded red brick and white
Moated Tudor Hall. A willow weeps where
Ducks splash in green. The high hedge is alight
With the last sunshine in the languid air.

I peer through an arch at the rose-garden,
Cloven Pan, croquet lawn, budding chestnut.   10
Beyond the vegetable garden I then
Peep into the high cage where peacocks strut.
One fans his tail: false eyes like works of art.
The nuttery is dark but lilies glow
From H-shaped fishponds (or stews) where rudd dart
Down to the viewing mound and barn below.

I turn the ring on the studded front door
And stand in the mullioned Great Hall and gaze
At the ancient brick screened cross-passage floor.
Adam de Otteley in Crusade days,   20
The Cresseners and then the Gosnolds sat
On a raised dais in an earlier hall
And fed guests. John Gosnold the Second, at
Henry the Seventh's reign's start, beamed the far wall.

Robert the First rebuilt and carved "RG"
Round the now walled-up ancient entrance and
Added "RA" on beam brackets when he
Wed Agnes in 1506. His grand
Linenfold parlour wall-panels predate
The "hung linen" of Lavenham Guildhall   30
Built by his cousin. Heir to "R's" estate,
An old Robert the Third stares from his wall.

Upstairs in the Banquet Room "R" built, my
Bedroom, Robert the Third aged twenty-four,

Fair-haired, and his bride Ursula, sit high,
Naked, columned, between the arms they bore,
Gosnold and Naunton escutcheons, beside
A Green Man who blesses their flowered union
In 1559, mark of "R's" pride –
They moved in when he died some twelve years on.   40

I descend the stairs that are scratched and scored
By spurs Colonel Robert the Sixth wore at
The siege of Carlisle, where, Royalist, bored,
He survived nine months eating dog and rat.
He fought on the wrong side and was then fined
By Cromwell's men, who filled parts of the moat.
I gaze at the deed Robert the Seventh signed,
Which sold the lands. The Hall went like a coat.

No more bowls and cock-fighting, cheer and shout,
In the "Plahouse" under the Banquet Room.   50
For two centuries the Rebows let it out
To farmers who barely wielded a broom.
And so, miracle! much is still intact
And this Hall is a living monument
To a family who were at court, backed
It as JPs and had a landed bent.

Here Bartholomew's voyages were planned.
In 1602, funded by the Earl
Of Southampton, he reached Virginia and
Named Martha's Vineyard after his small girl,   60
And perhaps sat at this hearth with Shakespeare –
Who based Prospero's isle on his new world tale
Of springs, sassafras logs and Indians there:
Caliban knew the Vineyard Indians' trail?

Five years later he returned and founded
The first English-speaking settlement in

The US at Jamestown, which he then led
Until his death of swamp fever. A thin
Stockade had then colonised the US
Thirteen years before the *Mayflower*, a base   70
From which to chart America's progress.
The USA began round this fireplace.

And now I am custodian of these beams,
Part of our manorial heritage at
One of Britain's top twenty (so it seems)
Historical houses, I am glad that,
Instead of sailing abstractly across
An unseen past of submerged homes and art,
I have found actual ancient rooms to toss
And anchor in as I voyage the heart.   80

The mind is larger than uncharted seas
And I have always been a voyager.
History is vaster than five continents' trees;
We grow in woods and make a Hall's timber.
The literary night flits with ghosts that
Loom and retreat, and I am glad the days
Have brought me to a room where de Vere sat
With Southampton to plot empires – and plays?

Night. I leave my gabled chimneys and grasp
Timber-framed Tradition shuts out a crowd   90
Of brilliant stars. I look upwards and gasp
For this year's comet, Hale-Bopp, trails a cloud
Of bright gas that might cool to fragments, bump
And cluster in galaxies. One pace, mark,
And Tradition's chimneys obscure its clump
With age-old warmth and shelter from the dark.

At Raleigh's Sherborne

I

We drive past stables and park near the gate
And gaze at the four turrets Raleigh made,
Blank out the wings the Digbys built as late.
The archivist takes us into the shade,
A tall willowy girl who smiles and knows
About the solarium's Tudor ceiling
Embellished with oak leaves, acorn and rose.
I glimpse the deer park, hear Raleigh hunting.

The archivist explains, Sir Walter leased
The whole estate, the Bishop of Salisbury's,   10
After he saw it, riding from the east,
From London to Plymouth where part of his
Fleet lay at anchor, with the Queen's help. He
Was thrown into the Tower – the Queen was fraught –
For wedding Bess Throckmorton secretly,
Came to the Old Castle exiled from court.

He squared arched windows in the Gatehouse tower,
Demolished the Great Hall and the south range
To improve views of his deer park and power.
Bess found the place draughty. Restless for change,   20
Two years on he rebuilt this Lodge, adding
Spanish top and turrets, held it nine years
Till, in the Tower again for pillaging
From Spain, he lost it, eyes brimming with tears,

When a clerical error in the deed
Invalidated his gift to his son.
We pass upstairs through drawing-rooms and heed
Ceilings where Raleigh's five-lozenged shells stun,
Linger where his great bed stood, silk-hung straw.
Then the archivist beckons and we creep   30

Up a roped-off stairway, unlock a door:
Apartments where the public must not peep.

We cross boards to a triangular room,
Raleigh's bare study: a Tudor hearth where
Side columns taper downwards. Here in gloom
By a fire Sir Humphrey Gilbert sat near
Hariot and John Dee, magician, sipped wine
And probed the universe in a great search,
Sought for other dimensions like Einstein
Or Koestler and questioned the rigid Church.   40

What happened in this turret? Gossips told
Of pacts with the Devil, a "School of Night"
That conjured spirits, trysts when Dee would hold
Black Magic rituals here in this hearth's light
Which led to a Cerne Abbas enquiry
Into Raleigh's "atheism", which would
Have meant "unorthodoxy", "blasphemy":
"Supernatural" means what's not understood.

I stand in his private bedroom and scan
The deer park for how he felt on the grass,   50
Exiled here after a rise that began
When he diamond-scratched on the palace glass,
"Fain would I climb, yet I fear to fall," broke,
And the Queen scratched back, "If thy heart fail thee,
Climb not at all," and he then laid his cloak
On a puddle so she tripped with dry glee.

I think how he colonised the US
At Roanoke, of his patent to commit
To his chests all Virginian *largesse*,
How, replaced by Essex as favourite,   60
Now a Dorset philosopher-poet,
He reached Guyana, wrote a book that sold,

Then trounced the Spanish fleet at Cadiz yet,
Wounded in a leg, limped, swashbuckling-old.

We peer at other rooms, dingy with dust,
Then climb his wooden staircase to the roof's
High balustrade among stone beasts that thrust
Into the sky (bears, dragons with strange hoofs)
And look across the lake at the old keep,
Descend to his kitchens, where ovens, raked   70
Ash from lit ash faggots in a hot heap,
Heated bread and pies put in to be baked.

In an exhibition I see the pipe
He smoked before his execution, carved
With two Indians and dogs, a native type.
I gaze at his portrait, not looking starved,
With beard, ruff, feather, painted in the Tower,
Labelled "Sᵗ Walter Rawleigh", for he spoke
Broad Devonshire. I see his Bess's bower
And from the courtyard wall scallop shells poke.   80

                    II
I bid the archivist farewell and walk
Round the lake to his seat where he surveyed
His gardens and looked at the road or chalk
Track to Dorchester, kept tabs on his trade.
Here he smoked his pipe, here his servant brought
Him ale and dowsed him, thinking him on fire.
I sit on his stone seat and catch his thought
As writer, entrepreneur, country squire.

In the Tower, under death sentence for three
Weeks in 1603, he wrote, aflame,   90
'The Passionate Man's Pilgrimage': "Give me
My Scallop shell of quiet"; and became
The oldest Metaphysical poet

Whose soul longed for an everlasting head,
Who brought in Donne and Marvell, calmly met
The axe-stroke he expected, and his dread.

During his next twelve years in the Tower
He wrote his *History of the World* and, freed,
Returned to Guyana for gold. His power
Was huge, the natives thought him king. One deed   100
Undid him – a Spanish settlement burned.
His son Walter was killed, he could not "buy"
A gold mine and was seized when he returned
By pro-Spanish James and sentenced to die.

I see the scaffold cleared. He takes off his
Hat, gown, doublet, with his thumb tries the blade,
Jokes, "This is sharp medicine and yet it is
A sure cure for all diseases." He's laid
His head on the block as on a pillow.
"Do you wish to face east?" asks the headsman.   110
He replies, "If the heart be right, it's no
Matter which way the head lies" – jauntier than

Friends, who begged him face Jerusalem. Then,
Asked "Will you be blindfolded?" he says, "Think
You I fear the shadow of the axe when
I fear not the axe itself?" and, one blink,
"When I stretch forth my hands, despatch me well."
He stretches, the headsman's overcome. "What
Dost thou fear? Strike, man, strike." Twice the axe falls.
His head rolls, shudders sweep the crowded spot.   120

I salute a most commercial fellow
Who cornered all Virginia's exports
And pioneered the sale of tobacco,
Contacting Indians from fortified forts,
A buccaneering sea-dog who through screens

Plundered the Spanish fleet, and, while rising
From a squire's second son to be the Queen's
Favourite, maintained his life-style by trading.

O Raleigh, you epitomised the blend
Of active man and contemplative eye: 130
Lawyer, soldier, seaman, architect, friend,
MP, courtier, entrepreneur and spy,
Explorer, businessman, publicist; yet
In the Tower scientist, historian,
Mystical philosopher and poet –
Supreme Renaissance universal man.

I identify with what you combined,
Entrepreneurial skill and mystic bent,
Panache in finding fine houses and mind,
Jaunty approach to death, poetic tent.   140
You knew the excitement of tossing seas
And the adventure of an enterprise
When all leave in one boat with a fair breeze,
Return with sassafras cargo as prize.

Most versatile and energetic soul,
You embodied the Renaissance ideal
Of seeing the universe as a whole,
Uniting disciplines in what is real.
You knew the coloniser's thrill and, first
Of the English, exploited the New World   150
And from your pregnant metaphysic burst
An infant unifying Age, still curled.

And now my metaphysic unifies
All disciplines – philosophy, physics,
History, religion, literature – likewise,
And through the measure of my odes can fix
Combined perceptions from all disciplines

In a *flower-de-luce* that embodies truth
And mirrors our structured Age's margins
As you mirrored its golden Tudor youth,   160

And reflects how a universe can sprout
And how the eternal grows into time
And how all civilisations leaf out
From a *cornucopia* always in prime,
Void that is known by still minds and brings storms,
And reveals how Providence works and strives
In the mystery of history's shape and forms
And in the outlines of our little lives

As a tangled yet patterned knot of lined
Leaves that cannot be cut like Gordian knot,   170
But must be grasped whole by reflecting mind
As enigma, riddle answering "What
Is life?", image which can be understood
When gazed at long by deepest mind and sought,
Whose truth can be glimpsed through its surface wood,
Truth that is seen but not reduced to thought;

As in Tudor gardens a knot unites
All box hedges and herbs, combines in one
Pattern a Fire that binds all things and Lights,
One invisible Being like a sun   180
That manifests into existence, seen
As multiplicity, different hedges,
But as one pattern when a peeping Queen
Peers from her chamber at the knot's edges.

On Curtius Leaping into the Earth

I
I sit in Otley Hall's ancient study,

Writing late at night. The dark shadows fall
Across the hearth's two-inch-brick weathered base.
Here a new wing without an outside wall
Was purpose-built with wood columns, once red,
To make an Elizabethan "Plahouse"
Where players came. This was their "tiring-room".
Costumed by curtains each peeped like a mouse

At gatehouse, drawbridge and a missing wing;
An enclosed courtyard where an old bell tolled.   10
Here came the Earl of Essex to dictate
Work to his secretary, Robert Gosnold
The Third. I see him sitting with his friends,
The players strut and bow, fine ladies gloat.
Essex applauds, Southampton at his side.
They are among friends, by the sunlit moat.

I see Essex sit in the Globe and watch
Southampton's *Richard the Second* and joke
At the treasonous message that a Queen
Can be deposed by a new Bolingbroke.   20
I see the running in the streets, the fear
Of Cecil that drove him to be displeased,
His dashed hope Smythe would send a thousand men.
I see his ashen face as he is seized.

Now, Raleigh Captain of the Guard, Essex
Kneels at the block, the axeman swings his axe.
It flashes in the sun, thuds through his neck.
The head rolls in silence, men turn their backs
And now the crowd drifts away. Most are shocked
At the bloodthirsty spectacle, disturbed   30
By this act of terror. I understand.
He leapt into the earth for his country.

Back here in this "Plahouse" the players weep.

Robert Gosnold sheds tears as an adept
Craftsman paints and inscribes how Curtius,
Now nickname for Essex, on his horse leapt
Into a chasm in the Forum and
Saved Rome from pestilence – the Cecils' sting.
A quarry in the Great Hall now proclaims,
"No mortal knows what all the hours will bring." 40

The players have departed. Civil war
Closed theatres, this one became a cockpit
Where squawking cocks were held until they fought
By Cavaliers whose spurs scratched the stairs. It
Hosted bowls, then was used as a cart-shed,
The epitaphs painted over in white.
And now, as the players' ghosts flit and smile,
I too mourn Essex in this fissured night.

II

A plague now blights our much-riven farmsteads.
Ill winds blow it from the south and the west. 50
Who is our Curtius today? Who has
Fallen on his sword to restore what's best?
Not Powell or Thatcher, who were destroyed by
Rockefellers' plan to break up our land.
No Owen has the stature of Essex,
None by an act of courage made *his* stand.

Tebbit, a man whose courage all respect
For being blown up by the Brighton bomb
When Russians, NUM and IRA
With Libyan cash tried to kill all guests from 60
The government, bring miner-Bolsheviks
To power under Scargill, and invite in
The Russian air force for protection, speaks
Out though in pain, wound weeping through chest skin.

⌐He sits beside me on a platform, late,
And writes his speech in two minutes, then speaks.
Now we lament our "United" Kingdom
Which has been fragmented into twelve cliques,
"Euro-regions". "We need an ELF,"
He says. "An English Liberation Front.   70
It's droll. The England of Montgomery
And Churchill's under foreign rule." I grunt.

We live among pygmies, our little men
Lack brave nobility, robes Essex wore,
To march against foreign abuse of power.
Are you the hero who will call out for
An English Liberation Front, and free
England from the world government's thrall, *us*,
By, glorious doomed gesture at pestilence,
Plunging into the earth like Curtius?   80

At Royal Sutton Hoo: Raedwald and the End of England

We approach the grassy plain with pillow mounds
And a high mound that towers above the rest
And walk along the bluff that overlooks
The River Deben way below. Distressed,
In the early seventh century soldiers dragged
On rollers an oak ship ninety foot long,
Weighing twenty-five tons, to be up high
On this ridge, near Valhalla, Odin's throng.

I stand between white survey posts and stare
At the square tape which marks the place where lay   10
The gold treasure of King Raedwald, the first
To unite the East Anglia of his day
And other regions into one Kingdom.
Converted in Kent by St Augustine,

He worshipped Christ but on his wife's advice
Kept an altar to the Devil – Odin.

Here England began, and the Crown Jewels
Of Angle-land's first monarch were dug up
The year of the war: Anglian royal wealth
On a scale unequalled in all Europe –   20
A sumptuous helmet fusing Roman
And Germanic styles, sceptre, harp and shield.
I stand in swarms of thunderflies and sense
The origin of England in this field.

Here in this royal cemetery there were
Twenty-one mounds of which Raedwald's was one.
I suspect the big mound Carver enlarged
To show how high the mound-piling was done
Holds the bones of Raedwald's father, Tyttla,
And that the cemetery at Snape nearby   30
Holds the remains of *his* father, Wuffa.
As with Ming tombs, here lies a dynasty.

Nearby I see replica shapes of men –
Wrists and legs tied, one hanged – executed
By Christians who hacked out their stomachs so
They could not sit and be resurrected.
One ploughman, killed because his crops failed, lies
Beside his plough. One has been beheaded.
They were buried in this pagan graveyard
As they were not Christians, though filled with dread.   40

Nearby is a mound to a cremation.
I think of Geatish Beowulf, who was burned
On a pyre in the ninth-century epic
Which East Anglians perhaps composed and learned,
Writing in Old English and in Anglia.
Was Beowulf based on Raedwald? Was the mere

Of Grendel the Deben? Do I now stand
On Beowulf's tomb? Was his great gold-hoard here?

The ship burial is similar to one
In Swedish Uppsala. Did Geatish thought   50
Pass to Frisia and Jutland, whence Angles
Brought their ideas across sea to this court?
No, one aristocratic culture, known
In Sweden, Germany and England, rose
Perfect throughout Europe. A culture blooms
Like cow-parsley in all Europe's hedgerows.

From this window a clairvoyant saw ghosts
Of ancient soldiers circling Raedwald's mound
And urged the dig that discovered this King
Who united the English nation's ground.   60
Now we are again devolved regions as
Before Raedwald's time. From this window, friend,
I see armed ghosts circle his mound and mourn
Our ancient nation's calamitous end.

INDEXES

Dates of Poems
Dates of poems in *Visions of England*, in contents order

The Lone Sailsman in Exile	1961
Song of Three Thames-Daughters	1965
An Inner Home	13–16 October 1966; revised in 1968 (?)
Orpheus-Philoctetes at High Beach	10 November 1972
Orpheus-Prometheus in the Blackweir Region of Hell	18 November 1972
Flow: Moon and Sea	3–4 September 1971; revised 7 December 1972
Shooting	20 November 1972
A Green Country (from 'The Flight')	August 1970
Cold Men, A Cold Sky	1 December 1973
Yew	January 1974
Knight	27 January 1974
At Battle: A Violent Event, Serene Nature	23 February 1974
Closed	February 1974
Silent Pool	February 1974
Chased	24 February 1974
Arundel	25 July 1974
At Stoke D'Abernon	26 January 1974
Tattershall Castle	16 February 1974
High Beach Church	24 March 1974
Porthleven	10 August 1974
The Royal Observatory, Greenwich	19 August 1974
Loughton Methodist Church	19 August 1974
Our Lady of Victories	10 October 1974
Southwark Cathedral	On or soon after 2 February 1975
Pilgrims' Pavement	On or soon after 20 February 1975
A Thought for Winter, The Fertile Soil	

of Nature: January to June (From 'The Weed-Garden')	August 1975
At Roche Chapel	On or soon after 10 August 1975
Lightning over Polruan	On or soon after 5 August 1975
Trenarren	On or soon after 10 August 1975
Arthur's Innocence	On or soon after 6 August 1975
Ghost Town	1975/1976
Energy Techniques	1975/1976
Wistful Time Travellers	26–28 April 1976
A Metaphysical in Marvell's Garden	24, 28–29 October 1973; revised 4, 16–17 February 1980
A Crocus in the Churchyard	24 March 1974; revised 17 February 1980
Pear-Ripening House	4 August 1974; revised 23 March, mid-April, 26 May 1980
Clouded-Ground Pond	4 August 1974; revised 23 March 1980
Time and Eternity	14 November 1972; revised 21–22 June 1980
A Stonemason's Flower-Bowl	24 July 1974; revised 10 August 1974, 19–20 April 1980
Beauty and Angelhood	1: May, 31 July 1981
	2: June, 1 August 1981
	3: June, 2 August 1981
	4: 21–22 July, 2–3 August 1981
Crab-Fishing on a Boundless Deep	24 August 1981; revised 19–20 April 1985
The Royal Masonic Hospital: The Nut within the Sun	16 September 1981; revised 4 October 1993
At Penquite House, Near St Sampson's	18–19 August 1983; revised 27 September 1993
Copped Hall	30 May 1984; revised 19 September 1993
At Hatfield House	Summer 1984 (?); revised 18 January 1994
Greenfield	3, 10 August 1984

Iona: Silence	7 August 1984; revised 18 April 1985
At Tintagel: St Juliot and Merlin	22 August 1984; revised 16 January 1994
At West Ham: Saved by an Artist	8–9 September 1984; revised 30 November 1994
Rainbow Land	August 1984 (?); revised 17 January 1994
Worthing	30 May 1985; revised 22 November 1993
Rough Stones like Monks	17 August 1985; revised 22 November 1993
Oaklands: Oak Tree	August 1985 (?); revised 14 September 1993
With Harold at Waltham	7–9 September 1985
Greensted Church: Martyr	September 1985 (?); revised 22 November 1993
At Dark-Age Jorvik: The Light of Civilisation	26 October 1985; revised 12–13 November 1993
Question Mark Over the West	16 March 1986; revised 23–24 October 1993
Cotswolds: Winter Four-Sidedness	22 March 1986; revised 29 November 1993
Ode: Counter-Renaissance	5–6 April 1986; revised 20 September 1993
At Cartmel Priory	18 April 1986; revised 18–19 October 1993
Castles in the Air	26 May 1986; revised 11 October 1993
Bluebell Wood	Summer 1986; revised 14 December 1993
At Gunwalloe: The *Tao*	16 August 1986
In Gough's Cavern, Cheddar	25 October 1986; revised 14 December 1993
By the Chalice Well, Glastonbury	26 October 1986
The Romantic Revolution	26 October 1986; revised 14

	December 1993
Gog and Magog	26 October 1986; revised 14 December 1993
Hedgehog in the Wild	Autumn 1986; revised 14 December 1993
St Olaf's Church	12 April 1987; revised 13 December 1993
Full Moon on the Pennines	13 April 1987; revised 13 December 1993
A Viking Inheritance	3 August 1987; revised 23 November 1993
From the Cobb, Lyme Regis	11 April 1988; revised 21 November 1993
The Dead Poet Bids Farewell to his Mourners	Undated 1988; revised 21 November 1993
Being's Shout	Spring 1989 (?); revised 19 October 1993
Elemental Sea	16 December 1989
Stillness and Tides	19 December 1989
A Man of Winds and Tides	20 December 1989
Snow, Peace	8 February 1991
At Polruan Blockhouse: Soul and Body	20 July 1991
Tall-Masted Ships and Woodpeckers	31 July 1991
Smeaton's Tower and Western Civilisation	On or soon after 17 August 1991
Mermaid of Zennor	23 August 1991
Copper Beech: Fountain and Fire	November 1991; revised 13 December 1993
Reflection and Reality	19 February 1992
Time and the Timeless	28 August 1992
Tin-Mine Near Land's End	29 August 1992
Transient Existence and Lasting Being	27 September 1992
Leaves like Memories	25 October 1992
Split Ash	1 November 1992
Flow and Flood	18 December 1992

Harbour-master	18 December 1992
Rain Globes	29 January 1993
Long-Tailed Field Mouse	29 March 1993
Poet and Snail	31 May 1993
Sea-Shanty	14 August 1993
Midnight Sky: Hawthorn and Almond	15 August 1993
Invisible Tree	22 October 1993
Peering Face	23 October 1993
At Otley: Timber-Framed Tradition	8–9 April 1997
At Raleigh's Sherborne	1–21 June 1997
On Curtius Leaping into the Earth	22–26 December 1998
At Royal Sutton Hoo: Raedwald and the End of England	9 May 1999; revised 17 May 1999

Index of Titles

(Poems in alphabetical order)

BOOKS

O-BOOKS

O is a symbol of the world, of oneness and unity; this eye represents knowledge and insight.